L. E. (Lucius Eugene) Chittenden

The Capture Of Ticonderoga

L. E. (Lucius Eugene) Chittenden

The Capture Of Ticonderoga

ISBN/EAN: 9783742865120

Manufactured in Europe, USA, Canada, Australia, Japa

Cover: Foto ©ninafisch / pixelio.de

Manufactured and distributed by brebook publishing software (www.brebook.com)

L. E. (Lucius Eugene) Chittenden

The Capture Of Ticonderoga

THE CAPTURE OF TICONDEROGA.

ANNUAL ADDRESS

BEFORE THE

VERMONT

HISTORICAL SOCIETY

DELIVERED AT

MONTPELIER, VT.,

ON TUESDAY EVENING, OCTOBER 8, 1872.

BY HON. LUCIUS E. CHITTENDEN.

RUTLAND:
TUTTLE & COMPANY, PRINTERS.
1872.

THE following Joint Resolution was adopted by the Senate and House of Representatives, at their biennial session, 1872:

Resolved by the Senate and House of Representatives, That the Secretary of the Senate be, and hereby is, directed to procure the printing of twenty-five hundred copies of the valuable and instructive address of the Hon. L. E. CHITTENDEN before the Vermont Historical Society, for the use of the General Assembly; that there be furnished to each member of the Senate and House of Representatives, three copies; to each Town Clerk, one copy; to each college and academy in this State, one copy; to each Judge of the Supreme Court, one copy; to the Governor, and each of the heads of departments, one copy; to the State Library, two hundred copies; and to the Vermont Historical Society, five hundred copies; such number of copies as shall remain after distribution as above, to be equally divided between the public libraries of the State, not otherwise supplied by this resolution, under the direction of the State Librarian.

The following letter was addressed to the Hon. L. E. Chittenden:

OFFICE OF THE SECRETARY OF THE SENATE,
MONTPELIER, VT., Oct. 16, 1872.

Dear Sir: By a Joint Resolution adopted by the Senate and House of Representatives, I am directed to procure the printing of the valuable and instructive address delivered by you before the Vermont Historical Society, at its annual meeting, at Montpelier, on the 8th instant.

I would respectfully ask that you furnish me with a copy of said address for publication.

I am, Sir, your very obedient servant,

M. B. CARPENTER, *Secretary of the Senate.*

To which the following reply was received:

25 WEST 38TH STREET, NEW YORK, Nov. 13, 1872.

My Dear Sir: I have received your note of the 16th ult., inclosing a copy of a Joint Resolution of the Legislature of Vermont, and requesting for publication a copy of my recent address before the Vermont Historical Society.

Although this address was prepared with no purpose of immediate publication, I do not feel at liberty to decline a request preferred in such courteous terms, which, perhaps, indicates an opinion of the Legislature that the paper may have some permanent value. I have the pleasure of complying with it, and transmit the copy, which you will receive with this letter.

Very truly, yours,

L. E. CHITTENDEN.

M. B. CARPENTER, Esq.,
   Secretary of the Senate, Montpelier, Vt.

INTRODUCTORY NOTE.

The following paper was read before the Vermont Historical Society, at a special meeting of its members, held at Ticonderoga, on the 18th of June, 1872, and was repeated, at the request of the Society, in the Hall of the House of Representatives, in Montpelier, on the 8th of the following October. In order to preserve the address in its original form, those portions which indicate its delivery on the ground where the events transpired, to which it refers, have not been changed, and it is now printed as first prepared. It was intended to print the letters and documents which are referred to, in full; but these are so numerous that only a few of the more important have been retained. But reference is made to all, and the effort has been made to refer the reader to the depositaries of all the known material evidence which bears upon the capture of Ticonderoga, in May, 1775.

The unwearied industry and perseverance of Mr. FORCE has brought many of these documents together in that monument of his research known as "The American Archives." To avoid frequent repetition of the title, unless special indication to the contrary is given, reference is made to the *Second Volume of the Fourth Series of the American Archives*, by the use, in the notes, of Mr. Force's name, without other addition.

Address.

TICONDEROGA—The lock to the Gate of the Country. It bars the entrance to the natural highway of Champlain, over which for generations swept the bloody tide of unrelenting war—a war so ancient that, when the white man first came thither, he found no living man who could tell of its beginning,—so continuous that its refluent wave rarely ceased its flow, until, one hundred and fifty years later, the great families who waged it had vanished from the earth, and peace spread her silvery wings over a new nation, celebrating its victory around the first altar of freedom erected on American shores.

Nature chooses all the theatres upon which the nations settle their controversies by the arbitrament of battle. They are few in number and limited in area. The plains of Greece, Northern Italy, the shores of the Rhine, the valleys of lower Virginia!—how many battles they have witnessed, what countless multitudes of warriors they have entombed! But not one of them has been the scene of war so prolonged, continuous, savage and cruel as that which ended with the Peace of Paris, which for centuries before had raged in the valley of Lake Champlain.

Its commencement was prehistoric. When, in 1609, the French explorer first undertook to penetrate this wilderness, the Indians of Canada told him it was the home of their hereditary enemies. Champlain gives us one glance at their fierce encounters, and the curtain falls for almost fifty years; though behind its folds we may still hear the war cry of the Savage and the shriek of his tortured prisoner. Then follows another century, the few but vivid records of which are gleaned from the relations of the Jesuit Fathers, whose history in New France is a marvel of missionary self-sacrifice and devotion. Finally, the contest becomes known as the French and Indian war, and thenceforward we have its written history.

The frontier which separated these two great aboriginal families was nearly coincident with that between the United States and Canada. The valleys of the St. Lawrence and the Ottawa comprised numerous tribes of brave, muscular, athletic warriors, who, for want of a better term, may be called Algonkins. Farther west, extending to the great lakes, lived the powerful Hurons, their friends and allies. Their enemies were the Iroquois, whose hunting grounds extended from the western slope of the Green Mountains to the southern shore of Lake Ontario. Their principal villages were in Central New York, in a line extended west from the south end of Lake George. History gives no account of a native race, surpassing the Iroquois in all the qualities which constitute the savage ideal of physical perfection. They were tall and erect in stature, their limbs were as active and strong as those of the trained athlete. It was their chief pride, next to skill and courage in battle, that they were insensible to pain, fatigue and hunger. The business of their lives was war against their northern enemies. To this they were educated from infancy. Their sports as well as their labors tended to their physical development. In their education nothing was omitted which could make them cruel, proud and brave, superior to physical hardship, insensible to tortures such as could only be devised by savage ingenuity. They constituted a great power among the native families. On the west, they conquered and annihilated the Erie nation, and swept over western Pennsylvania to the mountains of Virginia. On the north, they maintained unconquered a war of two hundred years. On the east, their neighbors sought safety in peace. No confederacy of native tribes, equally powerful, ever existed between the Atlantic and the Mississippi.

As in all wars, the fortunes of this sanguinary contest were variable. In the early part of the seventeenth century, victory appears to have been with the northern tribes, for they forced the Iroquois back from the outlet of Lake Champlain to the head waters of the Hudson. From this position the Iroquois villages were never again advanced. The Champlain valley was left a broad frontier, over which invading parties passed, and upon which they met in fierce encounter. In the absence of Indian towns, it became a nursery for game, through which the larger animals roamed in countless numbers. The reason is thus apparent why so few remains of Indian towns are found in western Vermont, and why the evidences of aboriginal occupation indicate routes or war paths instead of local stations.

Champlain made two visits to this valley, upon each occasion in company with a war party. Arrived at Quebec in 1609, he made an engagement with the Algonkins, that they should assist his discoveries in the country of the Iroquois, if he would assist them in their war "against that fierce people, who spared nothing that belonged to them."[1] In the singularly minute and truthful relation of his first expedition, he records the first meeting in this region between the opposing forces of barbarism and civilization. It occurred on the northern extremity of Crown Point, on the 29th of July, two hundred and sixty-three years ago.

The parties were large—the battle fierce—its fortunes wavering, when it was decided by the arquebuss of Champlain—the first report of a fire-arm which awoke the echoes of that valley.

---

[1] Champlain's Voyages, Ed. 1632, p. 134.

Before it, two Iroquois chiefs fell dead, a third mortally wounded. From the presence of a power to them supernatural, their warriors fled in terror, leaving a number of prisoners in the hands of Champlain's party. A new force had been introduced into their warfare, which in the end was to destroy both opposing parties. That night, on the Vermont shore, a few miles north of the battle-ground, they sacrificed a prisoner with tortures such as none but American Indians ever conceived.

There was a singular synchronism in the march of civilization upon both extremes of this great route of communication. In the same summer of Champlain's discovery, Hudson sailed up the river which bears his name. The French settlements at Montreal, and the Dutch at Albany, began at the same time and advanced with equal steps. These controlled the fortunes of the war. But the motives which brought the two nations hither were widely different. The conversion of the Indians to Catholicism invited the French; trade impelled the Dutch. It was the policy of the former to prevent the introduction of fire-arms, of the latter to encourage them. The effect was quickly apparent. The Iroquois, no longer content with resisting invasion, became invaders. I have not the time even to sketch the course of this war movement from 1635 to the end of that century. During that period, there was probably not a year in which a war party did not pass down the lake to Canada, and often a dozen were absent from their villages at the same time. They lay in ambush along the St. Lawrence, and returned triumphant with their spoils and prisoners. It was during this period that Father *Jogues* and other French missionaries, with numerous Algonkin converts, were carried up the lakes to the Iroquois towns, where they found their crowns of martyrdom with all its surroundings of savage cruelty.

At length the Canadian Indians and French were threatened with annihilation. To save their own lives, the French were driven to take part in the war. They armed the Indians, led their expeditions, and checked the Iroquois in their tide of victory. The southern tribes sought the same assistance from their English neighbors. The war was prosecuted by alternate invasions, until finally the quarrel merged in the great contest between the trans-Atlantic powers of England and France. Thenceforward, with seasons of peace on the Eastern Continent, the war here was almost continuous.

In all this warfare, Crown Point and Ticonderoga were the chief objective points. The temptation is strong to linger over its details, for its complete history has never been written, and we have not even a list of its battles. But I cannot even refer to all the events of the twenty years preceding the peace of Paris, which are necessary to illustrate the military importance of these positions, and to understand their connection with our own Revolution.

The final contest between the two great powers of Europe, for the control of the Champlain valley, became energetic in the year 1755. The English and the colonists had learned by a bloody experience that there could be no peace here until the French were driven from Crown Point and Ticonderoga, which they held with great tenacity as the initial stations of their barbarous incursions. Gen. William Johnson, in this year, undertook their capture, with an army of thirty-five hundred New England militia. The attempt was fruitless, though the fighting qualities of the colonists secured enough successes of the British arms, near Lake George, to make their commander a baronet. Had he exhibited capacity to command, the French might have been swept from this quarter in a single campaign. It was his fault that for many years " these forests were never free from secret dangers, and American scalps were strung together by the wakeful savage, for the adornment of his wigwam."[a]

---

[a] Bancroft, IV. p. 208.

The French made active preparation for defense. They called to this frontier the entire available force of the District of Montreal. By the end of August, when Johnson's army had reached Lake George, Dieskau, the French commander, had gathered here seven hundred regulars, sixteen hundred Canadians and six hundred savages. The impetuous Frenchman did not wait for an attack. Dashing forward to strike his inactive adversary, he mistook his route, and on the 7th of September found himself between Fort Edward and Lake George. He was just in time to form an ambush for a thousand colonists, who had been sent under Col. Ephraim Williams to relieve Fort Edward. Among the latter was the brave and venerable Hendrick, chief of the Six Nations, with two hundred of his braves. Led into the ambush, surrounded by invisible foes, defense was impossible, and Hendrick and Williams fell, with many of their men. Whiting, of Connecticut, extricated the remainder of the force, and with it retreated to Johnson's camp, fighting every step of the way.

The camp was not intrenched. Dieskau, whose motto was, "Boldness wins," dashed on, hoping to enter the camp with the fugitives. But he mistook the temper of the New England militia. Though abandoned by their commander, who left the field with the excuse of a slight wound at the commencement of the action, these marksmen of the woods not only checked the French assault, but for five hours poured into their ranks such a withering fire as they had never before encountered. The French regulars were annihilated. The Indians and Canadians, crouching in the bushes, kept out of the range of the fire. At length the Americans rushed over their slight works, and put the whole French army to flight. A French renegade wantonly shot down their intrepid and thrice-wounded commander. Among the privates of the American army in this action were Israel Putnam, of Connecticut, and John Stark, of New Hampshire.

The battle did not end with the fall of Dieskan. A body of three hundred New Hampshire men, commanded by McGinnis, crossing from the fort to the lake, just at nightfall, fell in with three hundred Canadians who were retreating in a body, attacked and dispersed them, capturing all their baggage. The victory was an expensive one, for it cost the life of their brave commander.

Instead of following up an enemy no longer capable of resistance, and capturing the forts here and at Crown Point, Johnson took his army to the foot of Lake George, and wasted the autumn in building a wooden fort, subsequently known as Fort William Henry. The French, whose power of recuperation, then as now, exceeded that of any other nation, profited by his inaction to fortify themselves at Ticonderoga. We shall see, hereafter, how costly to the American Colonies was this introduction of the waiting policy in war.

Although the year 1756 passed without any general engagement, almost every week witnessed a scout, an ambush, or a skirmish. The main body of the Americans remained near Fort William Henry, where, about the first of July, Shirley, who had succeeded Johnson, gave up the command to Abercrombie. During this summer, Montcalm arrived from France, hastened to this place, and assumed command of an army of about five thousand men. He did not here enter upon any active operations against the English; but, having made himself familiar with the locality, and greatly improved its defenses, hurried to Oswego, which, by an energetic attack, he captured. This year was signalized by the commencement of operations by the Rangers, under Rogers and Stark, who were constantly engaged in annoying the enemy and cutting off his detached parties. In the French market, English scalps produced sixty livres, or about twelve dollars, each; and English prisoners found a ready sale, in Canada, at sixty crowns.[9]

---

[9] I. Rogers' Journal, pp. 13–37.

The year 1757 is a noted one in the history of the valleys of Lakes George and Champlain. The Rangers held Fort William Henry through the winter, whence they kept up a succession of attacks upon the French. On the 15th of January, Stark and Rogers, with fifty privates, went from Fort Edward to William Henry, where they were joined by thirty-two officers and men. They proceeded down the lake, and flanking this place, struck Lake Champlain about midway between Ticonderoga and Crown Point. There they attacked a convoy of provisions, coming to this place on sledges. It was a successful, though rash act, for there were four times their number of Frenchmen in their rear. Learning from their prisoners the number of men at the two forts, Stark and Rogers at once set out on their return. Within a half mile of the shore, two hundred and fifty French and Indians fell upon them. Undismayed by superior numbers, they fought their way back to Lake George, and finally reached Fort William Henry, after a week's absence, and the loss of one-third of their party."[4]

The French retaliated. In March, a party of fifteen hundred, under the command of Vaudreuil, made the march from this place on snow-shoes, drawing their provisions on sleds, and attacked Fort William Henry, hoping to carry it by surprise. They were not successful, and were compelled to retire, after burning a few boats, some outbuildings, and inflicting other slight injuries upon the Americans.

A change in the character of this warfare, was now impending. The skillful, brave and energetic Montcalm assumed command of the French, and at once prepared for offensive operations. He began by thoroughly arousing the passions of thirty-three Indian tribes, which had been collected by the French Governor at Montreal. He secured their confidence,

---

[4] Rogers' Journal, p. 44.

by joining in their dances, singing their war songs, and they placed themselves unreservedly under his direction. With their excitement at the highest point, he set out with them for Ticonderoga. He reached this fort with the largest Indian war party ever collected upon the lake, numbering more than two hundred canoes. The precise number of men he collected here and at Crown Point, we do not know; but it more than four times outnumbered the American army to which it was opposed. Montcalm spent but little time in preparation,—long enough, however, to send out a scouting party toward Fort Edward, which returned with forty-two fresh-torn American scalps, and only one prisoner. These trophies excited the Indians to frenzy. Montcalm restrained them with difficulty. On the 24th July, twenty barges of Americans, under Colonel Parker, appeared on the lake. The Indians rushed upon them, took one hundred and sixty prisoners, killed and dispersed the rest of the force. The succeeding ten days were filled with events which I must pass over.

It must suffice to say, that on the second of August, Montcalm, with an army of eight thousand French and Indians, had surrounded Fort William Henry, defended by less than five hundred men within the fort, and seventeen hundred intrenched around it.

You know what a bloody tragedy ensued; how the gallant Monroe, who had only reached the fort the day previous, answered the summons to surrender with defiance; how for five days he held the place against the assailing host of mad devils, directed by French genius, while the pusillanimous Webb, with an army of five thousand men, lay trembling at Fort Edward, and answered his demands for assistance by advice to capitulate; how, when aware that Webb's letter had been intercepted by Montcalm, who thus knew that all his hope of help was cut off, he would not treat until half his guns were burst, and his ammunition was exhausted; how Montcalm, generous to so brave an enemy, granted him the liberal terms of marching his men, with their arms and baggage, under an escort to the nearest fort; how, after the surrender, the gallant Frenchman more than once periled his life to keep his agreement; and, finally, how his savage allies swung the relentless tomahawk against their defenseless prisoners, until they had reduced the army to a herd of six hundred fugitives under the sheltering guns of Fort Edward! It was, indeed, a bloody scene—too awful for description—the most cruel and devilish which these valleys, the battle-ground of centuries, have ever witnessed![5]

This campaign well nigh extinguished the English power on this frontier,—for, if Webb did not give up Fort Edward, it was because he was not attacked in his paralysis of fear. This shameful result was due not less to the cowardice of the English commanders, than to the dashing bravery of Montcalm. The Rangers alone declined to participate in the general trepidation. They hurried forward to the bloody ground, some of them within twenty-four hours of the massacre, and until the next spring, by a series of well-directed attacks, were a constant annoyance to the enemy.

A change in the British Ministry, which brought Mr. Pitt into the Cabinet, put new energy into the prosecution of the war in America, and, from the year 1758, affairs in the colonies began to assume a more favorable aspect. But, while British arms were everywhere else triumphant, the day of disaster in this quarter had not yet closed. In the season of 1758, three expeditions were undertaken against the French. One resulted in the capture of Louisburg; another in that of Fort du Quesne. We are concerned only with the third—the largest, the most promising—the only one unsuccessful.

---

[5] See Appendix 1.

The enthusiasm of the colonies, animated by the spirit of the home government, by the first of July, had collected upon the banks of Lake George the most numerous, best equipped, and most effective army theretofore mustered on American soil. It was composed of nine thousand Provincials, sixty-five hundred British regulars and six hundred rangers. Abercrombie was nominally at the head of the force, but its real commander was the young, brave and popular Lord Howe.

At early dawn, on the fifth of July, these soldiers, sixteen thousand in number, folded their tents and launched themselves on the placid bosom of Lake St. Sacrament. Their movement required a thousand boats, exclusive of the rafts which floated their artillery. The glorious pageant, decked with waving banners, cheered by the strains of martial music, moved slowly down the lake. As the rays of the morning sun flashed from their glistening bayonets and lit up the contrast between the scarlet uniforms of the regulars and the wealth of green in which the wilderness was clothed,—as their oars, with measured stroke, broke the surface of that lovely sheet of water, its lofty shores towered above such a military display as they never saw before—may never witness again. The living poem was complete, when, as the shades of evening fell, just beyond the place where the mountain slope descends below the surface of the waters, on a point named after the quiet of the Sabbath day, they landed and spread their couches for a few hours' repose.

The enemy they were moving to attack would have made a sorry show in the pageantry of war. In numbers it did not exceed thirty-seven hundred men. But they had been trained to war, and they were commanded by a master who knew how to avail himself of all his resources. He was even able to transfuse into each soldier enough of his own untiring activity to more than double his ordinary military value. On yonder height, he had built Fort Carillon. On the east, south and south-west, it was defended by the lake and river. On the north was a swamp, wet and impassable. There was only a space, a little more than a half mile broad, which Nature had left undefended; and across this he stretched, behind earthworks, his main line of defense.

Nor was this all. You need not read history to learn how the active Frenchman protected the approaches to his main line, for his works, now, after the lapse of more than a century, are nearly as perfect as they were the night before the battle. About a half mile in front of the narrowest neck of the peninsula, is a low ridge, sloping from the river towards the lake. Along this ridge he threw up a heavy earthwork, defended in front by a deep-dug ditch. Along the banks of the river and swamp, connecting this work with his main line, were small earth forts, which effectually defended him against an attack in flank. In front of the ridge, for the distance of a musket range, the trees had been felled with their tops outward, forming an abbatis, which was well nigh impassable. Still further up, at the river crossing, was a strong natural position, from which the river rounded northward to the landing like a bow, of which the road represents the string, intersecting the river a little below the head of the portage. The river crossing was held by three French regiments, with their pickets thrown forward to the landing; and a body of three hundred men, under Trapezee, was advanced into the woods on the western shore of Lake George.

Montcalm determined, early in the campaign, to fight the English at Ticonderoga. On the day an enemy of four times his strength was moving to attack him, he wrote to the Governor of Canada: "I have chosen to fight them on the heights of Carillon; and I shall beat them there, if they give me time to gain the position."[t] Montcalm commanded savages, and

---

[t] IV. Bancroft, p. 208.

caused massacres; but he was a brave soldier, and a true man cannot now write his name without a thrill of admiration.

Before midnight of the fifth, the English moved from Sabbath Day Point to a cove, about a mile above the outlet, protected by a point, which that morning took the name of Lord Howe. There they landed, and forming in four columns, began their march. As soon as they had left Sabbath Day Point, Montcalm ordered all his forces, which had been thrown out in advance, back into their intrenchments in front of Carillon. All obeyed except the detachment of Trapezec, which, falling back from its position on the western shore of the lake, lost its way, and for some hours wandered in the woods in search of the road across the portage. Meantime, the English were moving slowly forward, their columns jostling against each other, upon the rough ground, in the morning twilight. Near the outlet of Trout Brook, the right centre, commanded by Lord Howe, came in contact with Trapezec's party. Although they fought bravely, they were struck and crushed in a moment. It was an accidental skirmish, but one of those accidents which decide the fortunes of a campaign, for it cost the life of the gallant nobleman in command, who fell at the head of his column.

The fall of Lord Howe was the ruin of the expedition. With his death, order vanished—the *morale* of the army was destroyed. There was no force threatening his immediate front, and yet Abercrombie fell back to the landing, and thus gave Montcalm the precious hours he needed to complete his preparations.

I pass over details. On the morning of the eighth, the French commander was ready. Every man was in his station behind intrenchments, which the practiced eyes of Stark, and even some of the English officers, saw were too formidable to be carried by assault. Like Braddock, Abercrombie would not be advised by backwoodsmen. He moved in three columns straight on the centre of the French works. Braver men never rushed upon their fate; never was defence more successful. For three full hours, the grenadiers and the Highlanders hurled themselves against the wall of fire, only to be beaten back, and again to dash forward. Every point in the intrenchments was assaulted. Now they sought to turn the French left. The omnipresent Montcalm met them with his best men. They crowded around his right,—Montcalm was there to face them! Did an officer fall in the centre,—Montcalm was in presence until his place was supplied! The English did not make an impression even on the exterior line. The work was too close for artillery, but swivels and small arms condensed their discharges into a continuous roar, pouring a shower of leaden hail into an enemy at times not fifteen paces from their muzzles. But human energy could not achieve impossibilities. At length, beaten back at every point; entangled in the brushwood and fallen timber; melting, like a snow in June, before the withering fire; the English became so bewildered as to fire into each other. Abercrombie had hidden away where he could not be found. It was six o'clock in the evening, when two thousand men, the flower of the army, lay dead or wounded in front of the intrenchments, that the order was given for retreat, which, in a few moments, became flight in promiscuous disorder.

Had Howe lived, or Stark commanded, the English might have been rallied at the landing; their artillery have been placed on Mount Defiance, which they still held, and the French have been shelled out of their works. But Abercrombie was thoroughly beaten; and he gave no rest to his feet until he had placed the length of Lake George between himself and an enemy not strong enough to pursue him. He did not feel entirely safe until he had sent his artillery and ammunition to Albany.

During the remainder of the season, the French were alert, the English inactive. There were numerous skirmishes in which the French were usually victors. Putnam was captured, and only saved from the stake by the interference of a French officer. November brought Amherst, the conqueror of Louisburg; and when he assumed the command the long season of English disaster came to an end. "Abercrombie went home to England; was secured from censure, maligned the Americans, and afterwards assisted in Parliament to tax the witnesses of his pusillanimity."[7]

Successful as this campaign had been, it was the last substantial effort of the French to maintain their supremacy here. The vigilance of the English cruisers made reinforcements from France impossible, and the ceaseless activity of Montcalm had exhausted Canada of supplies and men. He wrote to his home government, that, without external assistance, Canada must fall; and his words were prophetic. The winter of 1758-9 brought its annual crop of scouts and skirmishes, which settled nothing. On the fifth of March, Rogers with three hundred and fifty men, came down to Sabbath Day Point, where, leaving a part of his force, he crossed South Bay to the eastern shore of Lake Champlain, and opposite Ticonderoga attacked and dispersed a working party of the enemy. He was pursued by two hundred and thirty French and Indians, a mile and a half, to a favorable position, where he gave battle, and defeated them. He then, with trifling loss, made his way back to Fort Edward.[8] The place of this fight cannot be definitely fixed from the account given by Rogers.

On the 21st of July, Amherst, having collected an army of eleven thousand men, passed down Lake George and landed on the eastern shore, near the outlet. Halting his main body, he sent forward a party of Rangers under Rogers, who attacked

---

[7] IV. Bancroft, 309.   [8] Rogers' Journal 129 to 134.

the French at the mills, drove them out, and held the position. The army then proceeded to invest Ticonderoga. The heroic Montcalm, who never recoiled in the presence of an enemy, was no longer here. He was on the Heights of Abraham, gathering up the last remnants of Canadian strength, to meet, not his master, but his peer, in a struggle in which both were doomed to fall. The siege here, began. For two days the French kept up a constant fire of cannon upon the English. But during the day of the 24th, the Rangers dragged three boats across the portage into Lake Champlain, intending to cut away the boom to the eastern shore, in order that the English boats might pass the fort, and cut off the French retreat. Before this could be accomplished, about nine o'clock in the evening of the 26th, the French sprung their mines, blew up the fort, rushed to their boats, and hastily retreated toward Crown Point. Rogers, with his Rangers, dashed upon them from the Vermont shore, and captured ten boats with fifty barrels of powder and a large quantity of baggage and supplies.

Amherst was slow and cautious. Instead of following up the French, he halted his army, and began to repair the fort. The Rangers were constantly scouting in the direction of the enemy. On the first of August, one of their parties returned with news that the French had abandoned Crown Point, without waiting to destroy it, and retreated down the lake. The lilies of France had floated over these waters for the last time.

The French retired to Isle Aux Noix, which they held with a force of thirty-five hundred men. Amherst remained here until October, engaged in fitting out a naval force, with which he intended to drive the enemy from the lake. When he finally moved, the weather was stormy, and winter was at hand. He succeeded in destroying the enemy's vessels at the north end of the lake, and then returned here into winter quarters.

Meantime, Rogers, with his Rangers had been sent upon an

expedition, which for its perseverance through hardship and privation, deserves a more full description than it can have in this connection. The Indians at the Trois Rivieres had long ravaged the northern frontiers with impunity, and Rogers undertook to chastise them for their savage barbarities. Leaving Crown Point on the 12th of September, he went to Missisquoi Bay, where, concealing his boats and provisions, he pushed forward his expedition. On the following day, he was overtaken by the guards left to watch the boats, with information that a party of four hundred French and Indians had captured his boats, and were following him in hot pursuit. Without halting, he detached a party and sent it back to Amherst, with directions to send provisions across the mountains to the mouth of White River, by which route he promptly determined to return. Outmarching his pursuers, he reached the Indian village on the 4th of October, and found the Indians engaged in a scalp dance. The sight of some hundreds of American scalps, displayed on poles, did not greatly dispose the hearts of the Rangers to mercy. Adopting the Indian practice, they attacked the village in the gray of the morning, and out of three hundred savages, slew two hundred and captured twenty. Returning by the Coos route, after great suffering and almost in a starving condition, Rogers and his party finally reached Crown Point with a loss of three officers and forty-six men.[*]

There was little fighting in this quarter during the next campaign—that of 1760. An expedition, under Haviland, moved down Lake Champlain, driving the French before it, with trifling resistance at Isle Aux Noix and St. Johns, until it met an army under Amherst, which came through Lake Ontario, down the St. Lawrence, and halted in front of Montreal. An army from Quebec had also reached the same point. The conquest of Canada was now completed. Montreal surrendered,

---

[*] Marault, Histoire des Abenakis, p. 489.

and thenceforward, until the peace of 1763, these solitudes were no longer vexed by savage or civilized warfare.

Ticonderoga next demands our attention in its relation to our own Revolution. It was the first fortified position won from British arms—its capture made revolution a necessity and independence sure. Vermonters maintain now, as they always have maintained, that this fort was captured by the Green Mountain Boys, commanded by their trusted leader, Ethan Allen. Within a few years, this claim has been questioned. The glory of this achievement has been sought to be awarded to an abandoned traitor. Without questioning the motives or the research of the advocates of Benedict Arnold, let us try here, to-day, upon the very ground itself, to put to rest finally and forever, the question—

WHO TOOK TICONDEROGA?

This question ought to be settled by evidence cotemporary with the act. Such evidence is subject to the legal rule, which makes admissible the acts and declarations of the parties immediately concerned, which, though subsequent to the capture, are so directly connected with it as to constitute a part of the *res gestæ*. When this evidence is all brought together and properly weighed, it is not impossible that doubts, which have been suggested by an imperfect examination of the subject, will disappear.

Let us first briefly notice one or two conditions applicable to this evidence.

The earnest controversy which had long existed between the settlers of the New Hampshire Grants and the leading officials of New York, not always free from scenes of violence and blood, some years before the battle of Lexington, had called into existence, upon the Grants, an effective military organization known by the name of the Green Mountain Boys. Many of these settlers were old soldiers, who became acquained with the attractions of the country when they were Provincials or Rangers, under Putnam, Stark and Rogers. Their colonel and leader was Ethan Allen. They were formed into a regiment as early as 1771. We can now trace the existence of five companies, each formed in its own locality, and there were doubtless others. Seth Warner was captain of the Bennington company, which was organized in 1764.[10] Remember Baker was captain of the company raised in Arlington; Robert Cochran of the Rupert company, and Gideon Warren of that raised in Sunderland and vicinity.[11] Another, raised near the New York line, was commanded by Dr. Ebenezer Marvin, of Stillwater.[12] These and other companies were well equipped, officered and drilled. They knew the value of discipline and prompt obedience. They were raised, not for holiday display, but to defend their homes and property. The promptness with which they obeyed the call of their leaders is illustrated in the pursuit and rescue of Baker from his captors, in March, 1772.

Having no legally organized government, these settlers gave the direction of their civil affairs into the hands of small body of their wisest men, which was first known as the "Grand Committee," and later, as "The Council of Safety." This body exercised all the executive powers of a State government, for many years. Its sessions were frequent; and, before the Revolution, were usually held at Bennington. It is safe to say,

---

[10] Hemmenway's Gazetteer, Vol. I., p. 143.
[11] Ira Allen's Hist. Vt., p. 26.; Hall's Early Hist. Vt., pp. 128-137.
[12] Hemmenway's Gaz., Vol. II., Tit. Franklin.

that in the year 1775, the Grants had as efficient a civil government as any of the colonies; and, assuredly, no colony had a more thorough military organization. In the light of these well authenticated facts, the evidence bearing upon the question before us must be considered. It is obvious that they will exercise considerable influence upon its solution.

With few exceptions, these settlers were New England men —attached to her institutions, intrenched in her habits—warm disciples of the doctrine of self-government. The same fuel which fed the fires of liberty in Fanueil Hall was abundant on the Grants. We shall see hereafter that the call for resistance to oppression nowhere met with a more hearty, unanimous response than from the pioneers among the Green Mountains.

It was to such a people, *thus organized*, that John Brown, of Pittsfield, came, late in February, 1775, on his way to Canada. On the 15th of that month, the Congress of Massachusetts, impressed with the necessity of keeping the Canadians and Indians neutral, if they could not be won to the popular cause in the struggle which they knew was near; by resolution, directed their committee to open a correspondence to that end. The committee sent Mr. Brown upon the mission, and furnished him with letters and documents to promote his success. Pittsfield was not a half day's ride from Bennington, where Allen lived and the Grand Committee held its sessions. It was the principal town upon the great route of emigration to the Grants. Its patriotic minister bore Allen's name, and was his friend. Communication between these two towns was frequent, and the condition of affairs upon the Grants must have been well known to Brown and his neighbors. He acted promptly upon that knowledge. He delayed long enough to visit Albany, and put himself in communication with Dr. Young, and then took the shortest route, across the Grants, to Canada. It was a part of his business to "establish a reliable means of communication *through the Grants.*" That he was in close relations with the leaders, we know, for one of them became his guide to Canada. This was Peleg Sunderland,[13] one of the eight whom the officials of New York had outlawed and condemned to death, without the trouble of arrest, or the expense of a trial. He was sent to inform himself of the feeling of the people, and he must have met Colonel Allen, consulted with the Grand Committee, and have known of the organization, for he declares that the Green Mountain Boys *had undertaken* to capture Ticonderoga. Satisfied with the condition of affairs on the Grants, he forced his way through many difficulties to Canada, made use of his two companions, one of whom had been a captive among them, to win over the Indians, and having executed his mission, on the 29th of March, writes an account of it, from Montreal, to Dr. Warren and Samuel Adams, the Massachusetts Committee, and, as if he were making a new and important suggestion, brought to his notice while on the Grants, says—

"One thing I must mention, to be kept a profound secret. The fort at *Ticonderoga* must be seized as soon as possible, should hostilities be committed by the King's troops. The people on the New Hampshire Grants *have engaged to do this business;* and, in my opinion, they are the most proper persons for this job. This will effectually curb this province, and all the troops that may be sent here."[14]

A moment's reflection makes the fact evident that the proposal to capture Ticonderoga probably came to Brown from, and was not by him suggested to, the people of the Grants. He communicated it to the Massachusetts Congress as a proper thing to be done, *because* he supposed it had not occurred to them. He wrote the letter after he had had an interview with the Vermonters, in which they "engaged to do this business." Had Brown thought of it *before* he visited the Grants, he would probably have spoken of it to his associates, and there would

---

[13] App. No. 3.   [14] App. No. 4.

have been no necessity for this communication. Which is the more probable, that the Vermonters, who lived in the vicinity, on an exposed frontier, which would be protected by the capture—who knew that Ticonderoga was the very "Gate of the Country" (and the only one), through which a hostile expedition from Canada could enter it—many of whom had been fighting through half a dozen campaigns to take it, should have been impressed with the necessity to themselves, as well as the colonies, of surprising these forts before they were reinforced, and should have seized the first opportunity through Brown of making its value known to the other colonies; or that Brown, a resident of Western Massachusetts, and a comparative stranger to the facts, should have made the suggestion to the Vermonters? There is nothing in Mr. Brown's letter indicating that the idea of the capture originated with him; and positive proof will be cited that it was first proposed by the Vermonters.

Nor is there the slightest evidence that the proposition of Mr. Brown received any attention in Massachusetts. That colony was fully occupied with its own concerns, for it was the central point of revolution. It had no time to devote to matters which directly concerned only this remote northern frontier. Although the letter of Mr. Brown shows that the capture of this fort was discussed among the Vermonters earlier than elsewhere, I do not regard the fact as of any considerable importance. In view of the impending contest, it may have occurred to thousands; it must have occurred to those who were acquainted with the value of the position in past wars. But they who organized the expedition, were ready to act at the proper time, and who finally made the capture, are entitled to the credit, although a multitude of others had spoken of the enterprise as desirable.

The next witness, in chronological order, is Ethan Allen. His full account of the condition of affairs upon the Grants, and the events which preceded the capture, *has not been cited by any of the numerous writers upon this subject.* A surprising omission, in view of the fact that his account was published when there was a half regiment of living witnesses, shortly after the event, and before any controversy in relation to it had arisen. It is found in Allen's " Vindication," as it is called, published in 1779, only four years after the capture.

This account not only throws light upon the question we are discussing, but it also proves the spontaneous loyalty of the Vermonters to the cause of liberty. It points out their vital interest in the coming revolution, for their controversy with the New Yorkers had just been submitted to the king and Privy Council, with every prospect of an early decision in their favor. It refers to their frontier, extended to the Province of Quebec, exposed to an enemy in possession of this fort and Crown Point, with a vessel of war upon the lake. "The battle of Lexington," says Allen, "almost distracted them, for interest inclined them to the royal side of the dispute, but the stronger impulses of affection to their country, impelled them to resent its wrongs;" and "the ties of consanguinity, similarity of religion and manners to New England, whence they had emigrated, weighed heavy in their deliberations." Moreover, they "believed the cause of the country to be just," and that " resistance to Great Britain had become the indispensable duty of a free people;" in short, he declares that their interest and their patriotism were directly opposed. He states that, " soon after the news of Lexington battle, the principal officers of the Green Mountain Boys, and other principal inhabitants, *were convened* at Bennington, and attempted to explore futurity, which was found to be unfathomable, and the scenes which have since taken place, then appeared to be precarious and uncertain;" but after consideration, it was "resolved to take an active part with the country, and thereby annihilate the old quarrel with

New York, by swallowing it up in the general conflict for liberty." I invite your special attention to what he says of Ticonderoga:

"But the enemy having the command of Lake Champlain and the garrisons contiguous to it, was ground of great uneasiness to those inhabitants who had extended their settlements on the river Otter Creek and Onion River, and along the east side of the lake aforesaid, who, in consequence of a war, would be under the power of the enemy. It was, therefore, projected to surprise the garrisons of Ticonderoga and Crown Point, with the armed vessel on the lake, and gain the command of that important pass; inasmuch as such an event would in a great measure secure those inhabitants from the enemy, obliging them to take post in Canada; but whether such a measure would be agreeable to Congress or not, they could not for certain determine. But it was apprehended that if these posts were not soon taken they would be strongly reinforced, and become impregnable to any attack, short of a regular seige, for which, at that time, the country was very deficient in the articles of artillery, &c."

"*While these matters were deliberating*, a committee from the Council of Connecticut *arrived at Bennington*, with advice and directions to carry into execution the surprise of those garrisons, and, if possible, to gain the command of the lake. Which was done without loss of time." [15]

We have here Allen's positive declaration that the Vermonters, who had the deepest interest in it, projected the capture of this fort, before the arrival of the gentlemen from Connecticut, and were only restrained from acting through fear of the disapproval of Congress. With this declaration before me, I think we carry the admission a little too far, when we say that "the honor of *devising* and putting the expedition in motion belongs to the gentlemen from Connecticut." A more strictly accurate statement of the fact, I think, would be that they set it in motion; but that the honor of devising the expedition, as well as its successful execution, belongs to the Green Mountain Boys.

Let us now inquire what was done in Connecticut by way of putting the expedition for the capture of Ticonderoga in motion; and incidentally meet the claim, once put forward by

---

[15] See App. No. 5.

Mr. Bancroft, but afterwards withdrawn, that the first impulse was given to it by Samuel Adams, when on his way to the meeting of Congress. The assertion has been made that in so doing, Mr. Adams was acting upon the suggestion of Mr. John Brown. But the claim is made by a writer of no authority, and who gives no authority for his statement. Colonel Samuel H. Parsons, of Connecticut, in a letter to Joseph Trumbull, of June 2, 1775, says [16] that on the 26th of April, on his way from Massachusetts to Hartford, he met Benedict Arnold, who gave him an account of the condition of Ticonderoga, and the number of cannon there. Arnold was on his way to Cambridge, with a company of volunteers. It does not appear that anything was said in that interview about the capture of this fort. But Colonel Parsons says, that he reached Hartford on the forenoon of April 27th (Thursday); that on his arrival, Colonel Sam. Wyllys, Mr. Deane and himself " first undertook and projected the taking of " Ticonderoga; and with the assistance of three other persons, procured money, men, &c., and sent them out on this expedition, without any consultation with the Assembly or others. The three other persons were Thomas Mumford, Christopher Leffingwell and Adam Babcock. The receipts signed by these gentlemen show that the next day (Friday, the 28th) they procured from the treasury three hundred pounds, which they promised to account for, to the satisfaction of the colony.[17] On the same 28th of April, they gave the money to Noah Phelps and Bernard Romans, who immediately started in the direction of the Grants. That Samuel Adams and Hancock had nothing to do with the project, is shown by Mr. Hancock's letter, dated at Worcester, Mass., on the 26th, in which he states his purpose to leave the next day;[18] and the statement of Mr. Wells, the biographer of Samuel Adams, that Adams and Hancock left Worcester in company,

---

[16] App. No. 6.   [17] Conn. Hist. Soc. Colls., Vol. I., p. 184, 185.
[18] Force's Archives 4th S., Vol. II., p. 401.

on the 27th, and were at Hartford, on the 29th. With the slow conveyances of those days, it is impossible that they should have reached Hartford before Phelps and Romans had left, with the money, on Friday.⁽¹⁾

From this time, we have the written account of the real director of the expedition, so far as Connecticut is concerned, whose particular and minute relation is confirmed by all the other testimony. It is the journal of Captain Edward Mott, who subsequently acted as the chairman of the committee having the enterprise in charge.

The journal of Captain Mott records his arrival at Hartford, and his interview with Messrs. Parsons, Deane and Leffingwell, on Friday, April 28th; their inquiry if he would undertake an expedition against Ticonderoga, and his affirmative reply. They regretted that he had not arrived one day sooner, for they had laid the plan, and sent off Phelps and Romans, with three hundred pounds in money, and authority to draw for more if needed; that they had gone by the way of Salisbury, where Mott could join them, and he received an order to have his voice in laying out the money. Mott readily accepted their offer, and with five companions started, on Saturday, the 29th of April. They reached Salisbury on the 30th; increased their company to sixteen, and on Monday, May 1st, went to Sheffield, whence they sent two of their number to Albany, "to ascertain the temper of the people." Monday night, they passed with Colonel Easton, in Pittsfield. There they "fell in company with John Brown, Esq., who had been at Canada and Ticonderoga about a month before." They "concluded to make known our (their) business to Colonel Easton and said Brown, and take their advice on the same." It is evident that their coming was unexpected to Brown and Easton, to whom their purpose was then first made known.

---

(1) See App. No. 7.

To avoid discovery, they had been advised not to raise their men until they reached the Grants; but Brown and Easton, in view of the scarcity of provisions and poverty of the people there, thought they had better raise a number of men sooner, and Easton offered to enlist some from his own regiment. To this they agreed; Easton and Brown joined them; the former went to Jericho and Williamstown, where he raised in all thirty-nine men, and got them ready to march. Easton and Mott then set out for Bennington, where they arrived the next day, probably as late as the 4th, perhaps the 5th of May. On their way, they met an express, who reported that the fort here was repaired; that the garrison had been reinforced, and was on being its guard; but, disregarding the account, they pressed forward.

At Bennington, they overtook the rest of their people, except Phelps and Mr. Hancock, who had gone forward to reconnoitre the fort, and the two not yet returned from Albany. There Romans left them, and "joined no more." "We were all glad," says Mott, "as he had been a trouble to us all the time he was with us." This Romans, is the "eminent engineer," recently brought forward by the admirers of Arnold, as one of the leading spirits of the expedition. He was a fit companion of Arnold, who finally quarreled himself out of the service before the close of the year.[20]

The journal of Captain Mott shows that the news from the fort was discussed at Bennington, but was considered unreliable. Mr. Halsey and Mr. Bull declared that "they would go back for no story, until they had seen the fort themselves." Finding provisions scarce, they sent Captain Stephens and Mr. Hewitt to Albany, to purchase and forward them as soon as possible. .

Guarding the roads to the west and northward, they proceeded to raise men as fast as they could, and on "Sunday, the

---

[20] Force's Archives, 4th S., Vol. 3, p. 1364-7.

7th of May, they all arrived at Castleton, the place we (they) had appointed for the men all to meet;" and on Monday, May 8th, "the committee all got together, to conclude in what manner we would proceed to accomplish our design, of which committee I (Mott) was chairman." After debating the various proposals, and what to do in the event of a repulse, they "resolved and voted" to despatch thirty men, under Captain Herrick, to Skenesborough, to seize Major Skene, his party and boats; and take the latter, on the following night, down the lake to Shoreham, to be in readiness to carry the detachment, on its arrival, across to Ticonderoga, where the rest of the men, one hundred and forty in number, were also to march the next day. Captain Douglas was to go to Crown Point, where his brother-in-law was, and endeavor, by some stratagem, to get possession of the king's boats, to assist in carrying over the men." "*It was further agreed that Colonel Ethan Allen should have the command of the party that should go against Ticonderoga, agreeable to my promise, made to the men when I engaged them to go, that they should be commanded by their own officers.*" "The whole plan," he continues, "was settled by a vote of the committee. In the evening, after the party to Skenesborough was drafted out, "Colonel Allen went to Mr. Wessel's, in Shoreham, to meet some men who were to come in there, having received his orders at what time he must be ready to take possession of the garrison of Ticonderoga."[91]

Leaving now the journal of Captain Mott, for the time, with the little patriot army taking a night's rest at Castleton, it may interest you to devote a few minutes to Allen's connection, up to this point, with the enterprise, and the circumstances under which his men were brought together.

The controversy with the land speculators of New York, then more than twelve years old, had brought Allen into public notice throughout the colonies. During the past year, he had been especially conspicuous. The land jobbers, who then controlled New York legislation, had proclaimed him an outlaw, and set a price upon his head. He had answered them with characteristic defiance. In the other colonies he was looked upon as a man of great energy, firmness and intrepidity, possessing all the qualities of an effective military leader. By the Vermonters, with whom he had rendered himself popular by many acts of unselfish generosity, he was regarded as a perfectly fearless enemy of every species of injustice and oppression. Few men in America then occupied a larger share of the public attention; there were none whose courage was less questionable.

The military organization of the Vermonters, with Allen as their colonel, and the evidence that they had projected the capture of this fort previous to the arrangement with Brown, in March, has already been mentioned. It may not be proved by direct evidence that all this was well known to Colonel Parsons and his associates in Connecticut; but I think a traverse jury would find that it was from the circumstances. Why, it may be asked; did not Parsons and his co-workers raise their force in Connecticut, or on their way, in Massachusetts? Why were Phelps and Romans sent straight to the Grants, with orders *not* to raise men until they reached there, if these facts were not well known to their principals? They went by way of Salisbury, the old home of Ethan Allen, where his two brothers, Levi and Heman, then lived. Their first act was to send Heman, as an express to Bennington, to inform Ethan of their coming; and Levi was the first man who joined the expedition. Mott and his party made a stop at Pittsfield. Here the Rev. Thomas Allen, the intimate friend of Ethan and John Brown, was the settled minister,[28] and here Brown, who

---

[28] See App. No. 9.

had returned from the Grants only a month before, where he had discussed the subject of the capture, joined them. When the Connecticut party reached Bennington, they found the officers of Allen's regiment actually in consultation upon the subject, with the Grand Committee, and only restrained from acting through fear of the disapproval of Congress. That the leader of the Green Mountain Boys should lead this expedition was the spontaneous thought of every one. Up to the night of May 8th, at Castleton, no other leader was thought of by anybody. An account published in the *Hartford Courant* of May 22d, not two weeks after the capture, speaks of the engagement of Brown and Easton by Mott, at Pittsfield, and says : " They likewise *immediately* despatched an express to the intrepid Colonel Ethan Allen, desiring him to be ready to join them with a party of his valiant Green Mountain Boys." A letter from Pittsfield, of May 4th, the day that Mott, Easton and Brown left there, refers to their departure, "expecting to be reinforced by a thousand men from the Grants above here, a post having *previously* taken his departure to inform Colonel Ethan Allen of the design, desiring him to hold his Green Mountain Boys in actual readiness."[23] Captain Elisha Phelps, in a letter of May 16th, writes : " When we left Hartford, our orders were *to repair to the Grants*, and raise an army of men. * * * We pursued to Bennington, *where we met Colonel Ethan Allen*, who was much pleased with the expedition."[24] Finally, Allen himself declares that, "the first systematical and bloody attempt at Lexington to enslave America, thoroughly electrified my mind, and fully determined me to take part with my country ; and while I was wishing for an opportunity to signalize myself in its behalf, *directions were privately sent to me* from the then Colony (now State) of Connecticut, to raise the Green Mountain Boys, and with them (if

---

[23] Force, Vol. II. p. 507. [24] Conn. Hist. Coll. 2, Vol. I., p. 175.

possible) to surprise and take the fortress, Ticonderoga. This enterprise I cheerfully undertook."[35]

Such evidence fills up the measure of proof beyond doubt, reasonable or otherwise, that the Vermonters were ready; that the men of Connecticut knew they were prepared; that Allen was the natural leader of the expedition. Against the solid wall of fact which it builds up, the detractors of Allen, the libellers of the Vermonters, the latter-day admirers of Benedict Arnold, will bring the little canons of their criticism to bear in vain. On this subject, I shall produce no other witnesses. "They who hear not Moses and the prophets, neither will they be persuaded, though one rose from the dead."

Vermonters! have you ever considered the circumstances under which this force was raised? Go back with me to these Grants in May, 1775. The Revolution has scarcely commenced; Independence is not yet declared; British tyranny is not here especially oppressive; British troops have not vexed this people. The country is a wilderness. So slight an impression has the axe of the settler made on the primeval forests, that one who saw them from a little distance would think they had never been touched by the hand of man. The stumps are undecayed in the oldest clearing; there is not here a city, town or village—scarcely a hamlet; for Bennington, the earliest Grant, has not had its church and country store for half a score of years. Instead of railways and turnpikes, there are foot-paths and lines of marked trees. A single road west of the Mountains leads up to the old route to Crown Point, and there is scarcely another. Mails and post-offices are unknown. Wagons and other wheeled vehicles are not yet introduced. Travel is on foot. It is the most recently settled section of the colonies.

Through this wilderness, from the Massachusetts line to the

Winooski River, there are scattered settlers. Each has located upon some share in a Grant, bought before his immigration, and this fact has located them widely apart. There is no State, county or town organization. All the government is purely voluntary. There are no binding laws; there is no power to enforce obedience to law. There are only the Grand Committee, Allen and the other leaders, and the Green Mountain Boys.

In this world's goods these settlers are very poor; they lack the necessaries of life. "The people on the Grants are in much distress for want of provisions," writes Captain Phelps, on the 6th of May. "There was great scarcity of provisions; the people are generally poor," says the journal of Captain Mott; and he relates how he sent his agents to Albany, to buy provisions, and forward them as soon as possible. Yes! they were poor enough, in all but love of liberty; in that, perhaps you are no richer to-day.

Can an army be raised under such conditions, among such a people? Not to resist an attack, but to make one, and that the first in a Revolution; to invade, and not to repel invasion. Not to defend the family and the fireside, but to engage in aggressive rebellion, in which failure brings the doom of treason to all; to capture, by force of arms, the first fort from Great Britain, once their mother country, henceforth to be their powerful, remorseless enemy; and all this with a celerity which must achieve success by a surprise? Who would not have answered: "In New York or Massachusetts, with their great cities, towns, civil organizations and dense populations, possibly yes; but here, on the New Hampshire Grants, in 1775, no; you state an impossibility!"

And yet that army was raised. On the ninth, certainly within ninety-six, and probably within seventy-two hours from Mott's arrival at Bennington, it was raised on these Grants, and counting detached parties, it stood three hundred strong, on the east shore of Lake Champlain, sixty miles away from the point of its origin, armed, equipped and officered, its plans all matured, ready to fall upon and capture Ticonderoga. How was this result accomplished ?

This question has never been satisfactorily answered. Those concerned were proud of their success, but seem not to have been aware that in the quickness of their gathering, or energy of their movements, there was anything extraordinary. They did not care to preserve the facts; and now the closest search reveals but little information on the subject. There is, however, one fact, briefly stated. Perhaps it is enough, for it illuminates the subject. From Castleton, Allen sent out a messenger to summon men to meet him at Shoreham, who *made a circuit of sixty miles in a single day.* He must have had a fleet horse, you will say; over such roads, through such forests, sixty miles was a long day's journey for any horseman. No ! Major Beach went, not on horseback, *but on foot*, from Castleton through Rutland, Pittsford, Brandon, Middlebury, Whiting, to Hand's Cove, in Shoreham, *in twenty-four hours*, summoning his men by the way.[*] Such a fact requires no comment. If such was their energy, even the raising of this army was a possibility.

Look at the picture ! Allen determines to undertake the enterprise. Instantly his messengers, stout of heart, and fleet of foot, bound away in all directions: over the mountains, through the deep forests and tangled brushwood, across rivers, up the hills and down into the valleys, to every cabin which is the home of a Green Mountain Boy ! Their stay is short; their words are few. "Allen summons; the meet is Shoreham; the business, Ti.; the time, now;" and he is off to the next settler, perhaps miles away. Brief, also, is the preparation.

---

[*] App. No. 10.

Allen knows they will not fail him; they know what Allen expects. Home, business, family, nor excuse, delays the farmer-soldier. The rifle, the bullet-pouch and powder-horn are always ready. The wife fills up the knapsack with provisions for the march; and, be it midnight or high noon, he is away, before the short prayer can be uttered for his safe return. See them, as they come, striding over the hills, winding along the mountain paths, down into the valley, to the one highway that leads northward! They have no uniforms; no strains of music animate their march. Not in ranks or by platoons, but by twos or threes or singly, with swift and steady step, they move towards the place of muster. Below every silent lip, beneath every buckskin jacket, is a great, patriotic heart. On the face of this revolving globe, there are no truer soldiers. Behold them, O ye warriors on paper, who would rob them and their leader of laurels bravely won! They are going to write history with their bayonets; to launch a new power among the nations into being! The Spirit of Liberty is abroad. On the mountain summit she is bathing her jubilant feet in the rising sunlight of a new-born nation's glory. She has sounded forth her summons to battle! These are her mountain children; this their answer to her bugle call!

We now return to Castleton. It is the evening of the 8th of May. The party has been drafted out and sent after Major Skene. Ethan Allen has gone to Shoreham. All the plans are settled; Easton is second, and Warner third in command. The weary soldiers are preparing for their needed rest. Now, there is the bustle of an arrival, and Benedict Arnold appears upon the scene. He is a colonel five days old--a stranger to every one of the party. His appearance is imposing. His new and unsoiled uniform gleams with golden splendor beneath his waving plume and sparkling epaulets. He is not alone.

No! He is "attended" by a servant—of the *genus, valet de chambre*—the only one in that camp, the first recorded appearance of the species in Vermont. To the soldiers of Ethan Allen he makes the cool proposal to take the command away from their old leader, and to elect himself chief of the expedition!

Genius of the grotesque! Did the pencil of caricature ever draw a more ludicrous picture? Does any man with a gleam of common sense, doubt how such men received such a proposition from Benedict Arnold?

In relation to this and subsequent events, the testimony is abundant. In addition to his journal, Captain Mott, the day after the capture, wrote a detailed account of the expedition to the Congress of Massachusetts. This document shows that when Arnold arrived, Allen had left Castleton, and did not see him until he went forward and overtook him the next morning. Mott himself was with the Skenesborough party, a mile and a half from the others, and was sent for when Arnold claimed the command. "We told him," writes Mott," that we could not surrender the command to him, as our people were raised on condition that they should be *commanded by their own officers.*" "We were extremely rejoiced to see that you agreed with us as to the expediency and importance of taking possession of those garrisons; but *were shockingly surprised* when Colonel Arnold presumed to contend for the command of those forces that we had raised." "But Mr. Arnold, after we had generously told him our whole plan, strenuously contended and insisted upon his right to command them and all their officers."[17]

Arnold's impudent pretensions, as might naturally be supposed, raised a storm of indignation among the soldiers. They "bred such a mutiny," continues Mott, that they "nearly

---

[17] See Mott's Journal, supra.

frustrated our whole design, as our men were for clubbing their firelocks and marching home;" but they were prevented by their officers. Mott, evidently, did not very well understand Allen's character, for when Arnold went forward to overtake him, his whole party followed, leaving all the provisions, " for fear he should prevail on Colonel Allen to resign the command;" and as he had to go back after the supplies, he did not again overtake them until the first party had crossed the lake. Arnold succeded no better with Allen than he had with his soldiers. That Allen did not put him under guard, or somewhere else, to suppress his pertinacious impudence, is proof that he deemed his claims too idle to merit any serious attention. It was necessary, however, for him to reason with his men. Mott states, that " Allen and Easton told them that he (Arnold) should not have the command of them; and if he had, their pay should be the same." Their answer showed that compensation had but little influence upon their view of the subject; for, says Mott, "they would damn their pay, and say they would not be commanded by any others but those they engaged with." Up to the arrival at Shoreham, it seems reasonably certain that Arnold was not *much* in command of the expedition, and it is equally clear that it had not yet been converted into that double-headed military monstrosity—a force with two commanders.

It has been supposed by many that the expedition followed the nearest route through Benson, to a point opposite the fort in Orwell. This supposition is incorrect. Leaving Castleton, it moved by the way of Sudbury, where it struck the old Crown Point road, and following that through Whiting, reached the lake shore at Hand's Cove in Shoreham, about two miles north of the fort on the other side. The distance by this route was about twenty-five miles, seven or eight farther than by the other. There were two reasons for taking it: it was farther from the lake, and there was less hazard of discovery, and it brought them to the shore in a wooded ravine, where they were perfectly sheltered from observation.[28]

The party arrived at Hand's Cove after nightfall on the ninth of May, strengthened by the addition of one hundred recruits. It has been stated that Arnold, failing to secure the command, had joined it as a volunteer. Of this I have found no evidence whatever. From his character, and what took place the next morning, it is more probable that he followed it, growling and disappointed.

Upon reaching the lake, they found no means of crossing. The party sent to Skenesborough, to bring the boats found there down the lake, had not arrived; there was no news from Captain Douglass, who had gone "to obtain some of the boats at Crown Point by stratagem." Allen could not send up the lake after boats without risking challenge from the fort. The chances of crossing that night seemed doubtful; the morning would bring discovery.

But Douglass had not failed, nor did Allen despair. There was a scow at Bridport, belonging to Mr. Smith, and Douglass went for it. On his way, he called at the house of Mr. Stone, in Bridport, to secure the assistance of one Chapman. The inmates were all at rest for the night; but two young Vermonters, James Wilcox and Joseph Tyler, aroused from their sleep in a chamber, overheard the conversation between Douglass and Chapman, and instantly formed the project of decoying on shore Major Skene's large row boat, which lay off Willow Point, on Smith's farm in the north-west corner of Bridport, nearly opposite Crown Point, in charge of a colored master, whose love for liquid comforts was universally understood. They dressed, seized their guns and a jug of "New England," hurried off, picking up four armed companions on

---

[28] Goodhue's Hist. Shoreham, p. 18.

their way to the shore. Hailing the boat, they offered to help row it to Shoreham. The persuasion of the jug was too much for the colored captain, and the story that they were on their way to join a hunting party waiting at Shoreham, allayed all his suspicions. The boat came over, started at once, and poor Jack and his two companions did not discover what kind of hunting was on foot, until they found themselves prisoners of war.[29]

This boat, and Douglass, with the scow, reached Hand's Cove about the same time, in the latter part of the night; other small boats had also been collected. Although every man was eager to be first across, the boats would not carry half the party. Allen and eighty-two men embarked; one hundred and eighty-seven, under Warner, were left behind. The heavily laden boats had to be rowed to the landing selected, a little north of another Willow Point, on the New York shore—a distance of nearly two miles. Here, just as the dawn began to light up the eastern horizon, they landed in silence, formed in three parallel lines, and sent back the boats for their companions.

Allen now takes up the story: "The day began to dawn, and I found myself under a necessity to attack the fort before the rear could cross the lake; and, as it was viewed hazardous, I harangued the officers and soldiers in the manner following: 'Friends and fellow soldiers! You have, for a number of years past, been a scourge and terror to arbitrary power. Your valo has been famed abroad, and acknowledged, as appears by the advice and orders to me (from the General Assembly of Connecticut) to surprise and take the garrison now before us. I now propose to advance before you, and, in person, conduct you through the wicket gate; for we must, this morning, either quit our pretensions to valor, or possess ourselves of this fortress

---

[29] App., No. 11.

in a few minutes; and, inasmuch as it is a desperate attempt (which none but the bravest men dare undertake), I do not urge it on any, contrary to his will. You that will undertake, voluntarily, poise your firelocks.'" [30]

Every man poises his musket. They face to the right young Beeman, who lives just opposite, who has passed much time at the Fort, who knows all its passages, buildings and quarters, is their guide. Allen heads the center file. "Forward!" is the word of command. Directed by Beeman, they follow Allen through a covered way to the gate. Here, a sentinel, confused by their approach, forgets to give the alarm, but aims his musket at Allen, and pulls the trigger. It misses fire. Allen rushes at him; he gives a shout, and retreats into the fort, under the shelter of a bomb-proof. The men press on inside the walls to the parade, where, facing the barracks, they form like regulars, and give three huzzas, which arouse the sleeping garrison. A guard thrusts at an officer of the invading force with his bayonet, and slightly wounds him. Allen strikes up the weapon, and deals a blow at the assailant's head. His life is saved by a comb, which turns the force of the blow; he drops his gun and asks for quarter. "Where is the officer in command!" thunders the leader. He is shown to a room on the second floor of the officers' quarters; he summons Captain Delaplace to come forth, or he will sacrifice the garrison. Aroused from his sleep, half naked and half stupified, clothes in hand, he appears, and, in reply to Allen's demand for instant surrender, asks, "By what authority?" "IN THE NAME OF THE GREAT JEHOVAH, AND THE CONTINENTAL CONGRESS!" is the answer. He hesitates. Of Congress, he knows but little. The demand is repeated. He submits, and orders his men to parade without arms, for he has given up the garrison. Meantime, the impatient Vermonters have beaten down the doors,

---

[30] Allen's Narrative, p. 2.

and captured half the enemy. Officers and men parade on the square; the cry of joyous triumph salutes the glad sun as it bursts over the eastern hills. Defiance and Independence roll back the echoing shouts of the sons of liberty. The first victory for freedom has been won; the first British fort has been captured, and Ticonderoga has surrendered to the hero of the Green Mountains!

The men left upon the eastern shore of the lake, less fortunate, but not less brave, led by the gallant Warner, now arrive to join in the triumph of their comrades. Doubtless, as Allen says, there was some "tossing of the flowing bowl," and the war whoop with which, according to one account, the assailants swarmed through the wicket and over the walls, was not wholly silenced by the surrender. Warner insists on his right to go at once and attack Crown Point. He sets off, and that fortress falls the next day.[81] The "Gate of the Country" is held by the sons of liberty. They have made that capture which, under the circumstances, was of greater value to the popular cause than any other that could have been made in all the colonies.

Since my purpose is the examination of disputed questions, rather than the presentation of familiar history, I proceed to the next piece of evidence which bears upon the point in controversy. Though one day later than the report of the "War Committee," it should be introduced here. It is Allen's letter to the Albany Committee, of May 11th,[82] in which occurs the expression: "I took the Fortress of Ticonderoga; Colonel Easton and his valiant soldiers greatly distinguished themselves. * * * Colonel Arnold *entered the fortress with me, side by side.*"

We left Arnold on the road to Shoreham, with his claim to

[81] App., No. 12.   [82] App., No. 13.

command repudiated by the officers and angry soldiers. His conduct could not have commended him to the favor of Allen, and yet, as the record has stood hitherto, Allen seems to have gone quite out of his way to assign him a prominent place in the attack, though careful, at the same time, to assert his own exclusive authority. Upon this expression in Allen's letter, the advocates of Arnold have, in great part, founded his claims.

It is obvious that Allen's expression has some explanation—that we have not had the whole story. So singular has this expression seemed, that some have thought the reference to Arnold an interpolation.

It is well, therefore, that the explanation has been furnished. Truth is always consistent with itself, and the explanation not only proves the exclusive character of Allen's command, but it presents the two men in their true characters. Allen, rough and unpolished, but with no jealousy in his heart towards the man who sought to deprive him of the only position he seems to have coveted; Arnold, conceited and imperious, so selfish, that he was willing to imperil success for his own advancement. The evidence now offered, throws light just where the story requires it. It is to be found in a modest town history—an example of a class of books now little prized, but which, in future times, will be preserved among the treasures of the historical collector.

The Rev. Josiah F. Goodhue was the compiler of a "History of the Town of Shoreham." He was long and well known in Western Vermont. For nearly a fourth of a century, he was the settled minister of that town, where his faithful service will long be held in grateful remembrance. Numbers who hear me, will testify to his many qualifications as a historian, and confirm my own opinions, based upon an acquaintance of thirty years. His judgment was cool and clear. Cautious, almost to incredulity, he was incapable of reaching a conclusion until it was fully supported by reliable testimony. A fact recorded by him, on the evidence of others, is a guaranty that the evidence existed, and that, in the opinion of a competent judge, it was reliable.

The account given by Mr. Goodhue of the expedition, previous to the crossing of the first detachment, does not differ from that of other authors. After stating that when the first party landed, "it began to be light," he continues:

"Allen therefore determined not to await the arrival of the rest of the men from the other side, but to push on immediately to the attack. When Allen gave the word of command to march forward, Arnold, contrary to the arrangement made at Castleton, interposed, and claimed his right to take command and lead the men, and swore that he would go into the fort first. Allen swore he should not, but that he himself would first enter. The dispute running high, Allen, turning to Amos Callender, of Shoreham, said: 'What shall I do with the d—d rascal? shall I put him under guard?' Callender, regretting such an occurrence at such a critical time, and feeling the importance of setting forward immediately, and of acting in perfect harmony, advised them to settle the difficulty by agreeing to enter the fort together. They both assented, and set forward under the guidance of a young man named Beeman, etc." His account of the entry and capture is the same as that given by Allen in his "Narrative."

Mr. Goodhue's authority for this relation is presented in these words: "These statements I had from Major Noah Callender, son of Amos Callender, who was with his father at the time." He gives the language of Allen's demand for the surrender, "By the Great Jehovah and the Continental Congress." Allen states it, "In the name of, etc,"

Referring to the time when his history was written, Mr. Goodhue speaks of Major Callender in these terms: "It was a happy circumstance that Major Noah Callender had not then passed away, whose memory, though he was then more than eighty years old, remained unimpaired. The author held frequent conversations with him, and noted down whatever he deemed important for the prosecution of his work, and it is with pleasure he is able to state that, on no important point, has he found Major Callender's statements to be erroneous, after having subjected them to the severest tests." This opinion of his character is supported by all his neighbors, among whom his long, industrious life was passed.

All the relations hitherto cited, bearing upon the claims of Arnold, have been silent as to everything which transpired between the departure from Castleton and the entry of the fort. The only occasion upon which Allen refers to him, is when writing to the Albany Committee. Mott and his associates, to whose authority all but Arnold promptly submitted, had definitely given Allen the command, by vote, before he left Castleton. The statement of Major Callender fills the *hiatus* in the evidence between Castleton and the entry of the fort, and shows that Arnold was permitted to enter the fort with Allen, to settle a dispute which the former had created, after the first party had landed, which threatened the success of the expedition. It also proves that Arnold's claim to command was rejected on the very eve of the entry. Allen's expression in his letter is explained in a manner which excludes the conclusion that he yielded the command to him in the slightest degree, and thus, the only evidence in Arnold's favor, except his own assertions, disappears from the historical record.[33]

On the same day, with his letter to Albany, Allen wrote an account of the capture of the fort to the Congress of Massachusetts. In the latter, he asserts that he captured the fort with a force of Green Mountain Boys, aided by soldiers from

---

[33] Goodhue's History of Shoreham, 12 to 15.

Massachusetts. He speaks in terms of warm commendation of Colonel Easton and Mr. Brown, but does not mention Arnold,—a singular omission, if Arnold participated in the command, when he was writing an official report to the authority from which the latter claimed to hold his commission.[34]

After the surrender, the proofs accumulate of Arnold's envy and disappointment. He could not be contented to yield to Allen the credit of the capture. "He again," says the journal of Captain Mott, "challenged the command, and insisted that he had a right to have it, *on which our soldiers again paraded, and declared they would go right home, for they would not be commanded by Arnold.* I told them they should not, and at length pacified them; and then reasoned with Arnold, and told him *as he had not raised any men, he could not expect to have the command of ours.* He still insisted, etc." In his letter, as chairman of the Committee of War, May 11th, Mott adds: "After the surrender, Arnold again assumed the command of the garrison, although he had not one man there, and demanded it of Colonel Allen, on which we gave Colonel Allen his orders, in writing, as followeth, viz.:

"To Colonel Ethan Allen:

Sir—Whereas, agreeable to the power and authority to us given by the Colony of Connecticut, we have appointed you to take command of a party of men, and reduce and take possession of the garrison of Ticonderoga and the dependencies; and, as you are now in possession of the same, you are hereby directed to keep the possession of said garrison for the use of the American Colonies, till you have further orders from the Colony of Connecticut, or from the Continental Congress.

Signed, per order of the Committee,
Ticonderoga, May 10, 1775.   EDWARD MOTT, *Chairman*."

In the same letter the Committee commend Colonel Easton as well qualified for a colonel's command in the field. They

---

[34] App., No. 14.

also "recommend John Brown, of Pittsfield, as an able counsellor, full of spirit and resolution," and "wish they may both be employed in the service of their country, equal to their merit."

The annoyance caused by Arnold's quarrelsome pertinacity is apparent from a letter, written on the day of the capture, to the Congress of Massachusetts, signed by James Easton, Epap. Bull, Edward Mott and Noah Phelps, as "Committee of War for the expedition against Ticonderoga and Crown Point."[35] It sets forth that, "previous to Arnold's arrival, the Committee had raised the force, marched it within a few miles of the fort," and, "this morning, at daybreak, took possession of said fort, and have given the command thereof into the hands of Colonel Ethan Allen. And said Arnold refuses to give up his command, which causes much difficulty; said Arnold not having enlisted one man, *neither do we know that he has, or could do it*. And as said Committee have raised the men, and are still raising supplies for the purpose of repairing said forts, taking the armed sloop, and defending this country and said forts, we think that said Arnold's further procedure in this matter highly inexpedient, both in regard to expense and defense." As these gentlemen were not acting under Massachusetts, nor bound to report to her Congress, this letter seems to have been written to induce Arnold's recall.

Colonel Allen's letter to Governor Trumbull, of May 15th, is next in order.[36] This letter does not mention Arnold's name, and it was carried by the detachment sent to Connecticut with the prisoners. "I make you a present," writes Allen, "of a major, a captain and two lieutenants, in the regular establishment of George the Third. I hope they may serve as ransoms for some of our friends at Boston." He announces his purpose to capture the royal sloop cruising on the lake; states that the

---

[35] Mott's Journal and Letter, supra.   [36] 1, Conn. H. S. Coll's., p. 178.

enterprise has been approved of by the Green Mountain Boys, and his confidence in its success, and subscribes himself, " At present, Commander of Ticonderoga."

On the 16th of May, a week after the capture, Captain Phelps addressed a letter from Skenesborough to the General Assembly of Connecticut, in which he recounts the progress of the expedition; the rendezvous at Castleton; the reconnoissance of the fort, and says: " On the 10th day of May instant, we took Fort Ticonderoga, and also Major Skene, and have sent them, with proper guards, to Hartford. There is, at the fort, about two hundred men,—in a fort of broken walls and gates, and but few cannon in order, and very much out of repair; *and in a great quarrel with Colonel Arnold, who shall command the fort*, even that some of the soldiers threaten the life of Colonel Arnold." * * " I also saw a young gentleman from Albany, that says they disapproved of our proceeding in taking the fort, in that we did not acquaint them of it before it was done. Perhaps it would be well if some gentleman should wait on the Congress at New York, so as to keep peace with them." [87]

It is in the highest degree improbable, that the cotemporary accounts should be erroneous in respect to the question of command. On the 17th of May, the " Spy," published at Worcester, Mass., contained an account of the expedition, which states that the men were raised by Colonels Allen and Easton, " agreeable to a plan formed in Connecticut." It relates the sending of one party of about thirty men to take Major Skene into custody; that the remainder crossed the lake in the night, landed about half a mile from said fortress, and at break of day, May 10th, made the assault with great intrepidity; our men darting like lightning upon the guards, gave them just time to snap two guns, before they took them prisoners. This

---

[87] App., No. 15.

was immediately followed by a reduction of the fort and its dependencies." In this account, the value of the captured property is given at not less than three hundred thousand pounds, or a million and a half of dollars. In this particular statement, there is no reference to Arnold.[38]

The captured officers were sent to Connecticut in charge of Messrs. Hickok, Halsey and Nichols, who reached Hartford on the 16th of May, with Allen's letter to Governor Trumbull, of the 12th, before cited. The remaining prisoners reached Hartford on Saturday, two days later, in charge of Epaphras Bull, a member of the committee of which Mott was chairman. The Hartford "Courant," published on the next Monday, contains an "Authentic account of the Fortress of Ticonderoga and Crown Point," in which it is stated that "*Colonel Allen, commanding the soldiery,* on Wednesday morning they surprised and took possession of the fortress." Governor Hall expresses what must be the conclusion of every impartial mind when he says: "This account, brought direct from Ticonderoga by the persons having charge of the prisoners, and who belonged to the party sent from Hartford with the expedition, is entitled to the character and credit of an official report.[39]

The man who should know best who his captor was, was the commander of Ticonderoga. He knew to whom he surrendered the fort, and who made the demand for its surrender. The singular arrangement of a divided command would have attracted the notice of a military officer. The evidence of Captain Delaplace, therefore, may well be regarded as conclusive. On the 24th of May, within two weeks of the event, he drew up a memorial for the release of himself and his captured companions. In this memorial, presented to the General Assembly of Connecticut on the day of its date, he says: "That on the morning of the 10th of May, the garrison of the

---

[38] App., No. 16.   [39] Hall's Address, p. 81,

Fortress of Ticonderoga, in the Province of New York, was surprised by a party of armed men, *under the command of one Ethan Allen*, consisting of about one hundred and fifty, who had taken such measures as effectually to surprise the same; that very little resistance could be made, and to whom your memorialists were obliged to surrender as prisoners; and, overpowered by a superior force, were disarmed, and *by said Allen* ordered immediately to be sent to Hartford." [40]

On the 18th of May, the New York journals published what was termed "An authentic account of the taking" of these forts. They describe the movement from Connecticut, the journey of Mott, Brown and Easton, and say: "The men were raised, and proceeded, as directed by said Mott and Phelps,— *Colonel Ethan Allen commanding the soldiery.*" This account does not refer to Arnold. At that time it was not supposed that Arnold would attempt to assert a claim to the actual command, whatever might have been his opinion of his right to it, as a question of conflicting authority.[41]

Upon what evidence, then, is the claim founded, that Arnold had any part in the origin of the expedition against Ticonderoga; or that he participated in the capture, otherwise than as an obstruction which imperilled its success? I think the answer must be, that it rests on the unsupported testimony of a single witness, unworthy of credit, habitually untruthful—as unreliable as was ever cited by a writer of history. That witness is Arnold himself. Your attention is invited to an examination of his evidence.

It will be remembered that Colonel Parsons met Arnold, and conversed with him about Ticonderoga, on the 26th of April. We do not know what passed in that interview, but, in the then impending excitement, it is improbable that its capture,

---

[40] App. 17. [41] See App. 18.

and its value to the colonies, should not have formed the subject of conversation. On the 30th, Arnold addressed a note to the Massachusetts Committee, describing the condition of the fort, but silent on the subject of its capture. On the second of May, the Committee appointed a sub-committee to confer with Arnold relative to a proposal made by him, for an attempt upon Ticonderoga; authorized him to appoint two field officers, captains, etc., and to dismiss them when he thought proper, and ordered the Committee of Supplies to furnish him with ten horses, to be employed on a special service. On the third, they commissioned him "Colonel and Commander-in-Chief over a body of men, not exceeding four hundred, to proceed with all expedition to the western parts of this and the neighboring colonies, where you are directed to enlist *those men, and, with them,* forthwith to march to the fort at Ticonderoga, and use your best endeavors to reduce the same," etc.[42]

It is obvious from this action of the Committee, that if Arnold suspected that an expedition was already on foot for the capture of this fort, he did not communicate his suspicions to the Committee. Their action looks to the raising of a force in western Massachusetts, the appointment of its officers, and the furnishing of its supplies. Nothing was further from the Committee's intention, than to give him the command of a force already raised, or to be raised, in another State, over which Massachusetts had no jurisdiction.

It has been commonly supposed that Arnold undertook, in good faith, to execute the instructions of the Committee; that he went to Berkshire, the western county of Massachusetts, and commenced his enlistments; but finding that an expedition had already started, left others to complete the work, and, himself, hurried on until he overtook the party at Castleton.

---

[42] Forces' Archives, 4th S., V. II., p. 750, 751.

This, I think, is an incorrect conclusion. *There is no evidence that he ever raised, or undertook to raise a man!* What he did do will be hereafter shown.

The distance from Cambridge to Rupert, Vermont, which he reached on the 8th of May, by the most direct route, was about one hundred and seventy-five miles. If he left Cambridge the day after his commisson bears date, his movements must have been undelayed, if he reached Rupert by the 8th. That he could have gone by the way of Pittsfield, stopping long enough to make arrangements for raising men, is highly improbable, for that would have added seventy-five miles to the length of his journey. If he went to western Massachusetts, he would certainly have gone to Pittsfield, for that was the principal town, and the headquarters of Colonel Easton's regiment. That he did not go there, is shown, I think, by the letter of the Rev. Thomas Allen to General Pomeroy, who, writing from Pittsfield on the 9th, the day after Arnold reached Castleton, says: "Since I wrote the last paragraph, an express has arrived from B. Arnold, Commander of the forces against Ticonderoga, for recruits." [43] Mr. Allen was one of the most active of the friends of liberty in Pittsfield. It is impossible that Arnold should have been in his town, enlisting men, three days before, without his knowledge.

Arnold's letter from Rupert, Vt., of May 8th, is directed to the gentlemen in the southern towns, and urges them to exert themselves, and to send forward as many men as they can possibly spare " to join the army here" It contains directions about their provisions, ammunition and blankets ; states their wages, which he engages " to see paid ; " and describes the number of men at the fort, and states what he desires to accomplish. [44] It is precisely such a letter as he would have written if he had not been to Pittsfield before, and states the facts which he

---

[43] App., No. 19.   [44] App., No. 20.

would have certainly communicated in person, if he had had the opportunity. The expression, "Commander of the forces," is the same *totidem verbis* with that used by Mr. Allen in his letter from Pittsfield, and renders it highly probable that this letter was brought by the express to which the Rev. Thomas Allen refers, as having arrived on the 9th from "B. Arnold, Commander of the forces," etc.

In view of these facts, in connection with Arnold's pertinacious repetition of his claim to the command, before and after the capture, his conduct may be more reasonably accounted for in another way. He suspected, perhaps knew, that Parsons would go to Hartford and get up the expedition. If Parsons intended to do what he did a few hours later, his purpose was formed before, or during, his interview with Arnold, and, as the latter was on his way to Cambridge, there was no reason why Parsons should conceal his purpose. Arnold also knew that secrecy would induce Parsons not to make his object known to the Assembly of Connecticut; that he would, therefore, have no *commission* from that body, and, upon the Grants, there was no recognized authority which could commission anybody. Arnold's plan to secure command of the expedition, and, in the event of success, the honor of the capture, only required a commission, as color of authority. Arrived at Cambridge, he applied to the Committee of Safety, represented the value of the fort, and the ease with which it could be taken; and the Committee, not aware that an expedition was on foot, having use at home for the forces already raised, readily commissioned him, on condition that he should raise his own men. Such a commission, Arnold thought, would serve his purpose, and, having obtained it, he pushed straight for the fort by the shortest and quickest route, sending an express to western Massachusetts, to enlist men. He knew that no officer in the party had any regular commission; if he could overtake it before the capture, he expected a ready submission. Others would have the labor, he the honor of the enterprise. This view explains his angry disappointment at the stern refusal which met his assertion of command, and his repeated claim that he alone had any legal authority. It is also confirmed by the fact, that not a man raised under Arnold's authority reached the fort until the 13th, as I shall show hereafter. If he began to raise recruits as early as the 6th or 7th of May, when so much depended upon expedition, some of them could have reached the fort in less than a week, with no obstructions in their way, if Ethan Allen could raise his army, march it about the same distance, gather up the scattered boats, cross the lake and capture Ticonderoga in less than five days.

The first document upon which Arnold's claim of actual command rests, is his letter to the Massachusetts Committee, dated May 11th, the day after the fort was taken.[1] He refers in this letter to one written the day before, in which he stated that, on his arrival in the vicinity, he found and joined a party, led by Allen, bound on the same errand with himself; that he decided *not to wait for the arrival of the troops he* " *had engaged on the road !* " That " we had taken the fort, etc.," of which he intended to keep possession until further advices. He asserts that " on and before our taking possession here, I had agreed with Colonel Allen to issue further orders jointly, until I could raise a sufficient number of men to relieve his people, since which, Colonel Allen, *finding he had the ascendancy over his people,* positively insisted I should have no command." " The power is now taken out of my hands, and I am not consulted; neither have I any voice in any matters."

This letter was written the day his express for men arrived at Pittsfield. He had not, at that time, a man " engaged." The Mott Committee were not aware that he had " raised one

[S] App., No. 21.

man;" and yet he writes as if his army was on the march, and its arrival expected in a short time. What had he to do with "deciding" upon the time when the attack should be made? He speaks of those who were to make it as Allen's "people," and yet he asserts an agreement *made with* Allen, "on and *before* taking possession," "to issue *further* orders jointly." Were there two agreements? Did they refer to orders *after* the fort was in possession of the Vermonters, or *previous* to the capture? It has been shown that Allen was not present when Arnold claimed the command, at Castleton; that the men would have nothing to do with him; that, when he pressed his claim, they were excited, almost to mutiny; that when he followed after Allen, Mott and his Committee pursued him, fearing that Allen might yield; that Allen refused to yield, and the men said they would not submit if he did! Where, then, was this *agreement* made? Arnold's answer is, "on and before the capture." Allen receded from it, "finding he had the ascendancy over his men." When was Allen in doubt about his relations to his men, and their wish that he should command them? Arnold's account will not bear analysis. There is an incoherence of time, place and circumstances in the statement of this agreement, which proves its own manufacture by a false witness. It is as absurd, considered in connection with the admitted facts, as the military novelty of an attacking force with two commanders, equal in rank and authority.

The same letter describes the soldiers, after the capture, as being in a state of anarchy—plundering private property, threatening desertion, and other enormities—and states that one hundred men would easily retake the place. Here, again, Arnold is contradicted by the facts. Had they been plundered, would Delaplace and his men have kept silence? In all their complaints, and they made many, there is no word of complaint against Allen and his men. With a single exception, Arnold is the only witness on this point, and the exception only proves that Arnold impressed one man, twenty days after the capture, with the idea that, but for Arnold, "people *would have been plundered* of their private property." There was no private property, except such as may have belonged to the inmates of the fort.

One statement in this letter is so palpably untrue, that it is difficult to conceive why even Arnold should have made it. He avers that the party " I advised were gone to Crown Point, are returned," and that expedition "is entirely laid aside." At the moment that letter was written, Crown Point *was actually in Warner's possession.*⁽⁴⁶⁾ Arnold probably knew the fact of its capture. He must have known that Warner and his party had gone to take it, and he knew he was penning a falsehood when he wrote that the expedition was laid aside. He admits that Allen is a proper man to head " his own wild people," but insists that he is ignorant of military science. His dissatisfaction is universal. Although *the power was taken out of his hands, and he had* " *no voice in any matters*," he " is determined to insist on his rights, and remain here against all opposition," as he "is the only person who has been *legally authorized* to take possession of this place." This expression confirms the committee's account, that he persisted in his claim to the command after he was repudiated by the entire party. Were there no other evidence than the statements of this angry letter, all fair men would pronounce Arnold's claim to participate in the command, as untrue as, in view of the facts, it was improbable.

On the 14th of May, Arnold again wrote the same Committee.⁽⁴⁷⁾ This letter recounts the insults he had suffered in the public service; declares that he has about one hundred men, and is expecting more; that the dispute between himself and Allen is subsiding; but contains no other reference to the subject of command. The material facts of this letter are all untrue. Arnold says: "*I ordered a party to Skenesborough, to take Major Skene, who have made him prisoner, and seized a small schooner, which has just arrived here.*" Skene was taken on the 9th of May, the day before the fort was captured. The capturing party, under Herrick, had been sent from Castleton before Arnold reached there. Two days before the date of this letter, Allen had sent Skene and Delaplace to Hartford, as prisoners of war. And yet Arnold writes, "*I* ordered the party," etc. And this statement convicts him of another falsehood. His express had reached Pittsfield on the 9th. Eighteen men each, were drafted from some of the companies of Colonel Easton's regiment, and *fifty* men thus raised, under Captains Brown and Oswald, arrived at Skenesborough on the 11th. They left in the schooner which Herrick had captured, and reached Ticonderoga on the 14th. They were the first men who came to Arnold, and they were only fifty in number, as Arnold himself states in his next letter of May 19th. He thus doubles their number, and reports to his superiors that he had originated the plan of capturing Skenesborough, and despatched the party, which had just returned, after successfully executing his plan. That the vessel arrived, is the only element of truth in the statement. The men who came on her had not been enlisted when Skenesborough was captured.

Arnold's next letter is dated at Crown Point, on the 19th of May. It expresses his fears "that some persons might attempt to injure him in the esteem of Congress," and his desire to be "superseded." It has no other reference to the main question. He announces the arrival of Brown and Oswald with *fifty* men, and repeats the false statement that they had taken possession of the schooner, at Skenesboro'. He also announces the capture of the royal sloop, at St. Johns, and Allen's departure for Canada.[18]

The Provincial Congress of Massachusetts gave little countenance to Arnold's assumptions. On the 16th of May, the Committee of Correspondence for Connecticut had written to the Massachusetts Congress, that the expedition had been set on foot by some private gentlemen of the former colony, who had made the capture before the Massachusetts party came up. Referring to the question of command which had arisen, the letter intimated that this, and all similar expeditions, should be regarded as undertaken for the common benefit of all the colonies, and that the present was no time to dispute about precedency.[16]

The action of Massachusetts upon the subject is consistent with her record. On the 17th of May, her Provincial Congress received the first information of the capture of Ticonderoga, not from Arnold, but from Colonel Allen and Edward Mott—the officer in command, and the chairman of the committee under whom he acted. Nor is this all. The letters containing the information were sent by Colonel Easton, who, it was stated in Allen's letter, commanded the Massachusetts men. Upon Easton's arrival with the letters, the Congress appointed one committee to report on the subject of the capture, and another to introduce Colonel Easton to the House, "to give a narrative of that transaction, and that each member have liberty to ask him any questions." The report of the committee was presented on the same day; it proposed a letter to Connecticut, and a preamble and resolution in the following terms:

"The Congress having received authentic intelligence that the fort at *Ticonderoga* is surrendered into the hands of

[18] Force Ib., p. 643.   [16] Force Ib., p. 618.

Colonel *Ethan Allen* and others, together with the artillery and the artillery stores, ammunition, etc., thereunto belonging, for the benefit of these colonies, occasioned by the intrepid valor of a number of men under the command of the said Colonel *Allen*, Colonel *Easton*, of the *Massachusetts*, and others; and by the advice and direction of the Committee for that Expedition, the said Colonel *Allen* is to remain in possession of the same, and its dependencies, until further orders.

"*Resolved,* That this Congress do highly approve of the same; and the General Assembly of the Colony of *Connecticut* are hereby desired to give directions relative to garrisoning and maintaining the same for the future, until the advice of the Continental Congress can be had in that behalf."

There was an additional resolution, asking Connecticut to give orders for the removal of some of the cannon to Massachusetts.[50]

It is submitted to the judgment of just men, whether this official action of the Congress of Massachusetts is not decisive against the claims now made in Arnold's behalf. This was the Congress to which Arnold should have officially reported the capture, if he made it; for he was acting under its authority, if he acted at all. He not only allows Allen to make this official report, and transmit it by Easton, but he contents himself with a complaining letter, upon general topics, to the Committee of Safety, consisting of a few members, and *never reports the capture to the Congress.* And this Congress, having Easton, the Colonel of one of their own regiments, the third in rank at Ticonderoga, before it, to give a narrative of the whole transaction, with liberty to each member to question him—upon the report of a special committee to consider the whole subject—adopts a resolution, which spreads upon its records the facts that the expedition was under the orders of a

---

[50] See Journals, Prov. Con. of Mass., for May 17, 1775.

committee; that Allen was in command, and that the fort was surrendered to him; that he is to remain in possession, and, finally, approving of the whole proceeding, *without making any reference, express or implied, to the man whom it is now claimed captured this fort under the authority of the very body which thus ignored him and his pretensions.*

In the letter to Connecticut, Arnold is mentioned in a manner which shows the anxiety of the Congress to be rid of him as quietly as possible. They suggest that Arnold should be sent to Massachusetts with some of the cannon, " with all possible haste," as "*a means of settling any disputes which may have arisen between him and some other officers.*" This is the only reference to Arnold in the proceedings of the Congress.[51]

The Committee of Safety, on the 22d of May, referred Arnold's letter, of the 11th, to the Congress, as relating to a subject beyond its own control. That body, on the same day, addressed a letter to Arnold, acknowledging the receipt of his, and applauding "*the conduct of the troops!*" It also "thanks him for his exertions in the cause," encloses a copy of the letter to Connecticut, and then proceeds to dispose of the whole subject, so far as Massachusetts was concerned, by the statement that, "as the affairs of that expedition began in the Colony of Connecticut, and the cause being common to us all, we have already wrote to the General Assembly of that Colony *to take the whole matter, respecting the same, under their care and direction,*" etc.[52]

This letter was a practical revocation of any authority which Massachusetts had conferred upon Arnold, and it was clearly his duty to have returned to the army at Cambridge; or to have sought his future directions from Connecticut. He did neither; but remained at Crown Point, where all his subse-

---

[51] Force, 807. See App. No. 24. [52] Force I., p. 689.

quent letters are dated. In a letter of May 23d, to the Committee of Safety, he calls for money and provisions, and indulges in ill-concealed exultation over Allen's failure to take Montreal.[53] Without waiting for any orders or permission from either Connecticut or New York to do so, on the 26th of May, he announces his purpose to send some of the captured cannon to Massachusetts. This lawless proceeding, intimated in a previous letter, called forth an apology from Massachusetts to New York, and an expression of the hope that it would be overlooked as a mistake made "in the hurry and confusion of war." [54]

Immediately after the capture of Ticonderoga, Allen had undertaken to impress upon the Colonies the importance of attacking the British forces in Canada, by the way of Lake Champlain. Day after day he despatched letters to the Continental, as well as the Provincial Congresses, and their influential members, in which he demonstrated the feasibility of the enterprise, which he declared he could accomplish with fifteen hundred men. But the Colonies were not yet ripe for measures of invasion. Instead of attacking Canada, they doubted whether they should hold Ticonderoga, which, in Allen's opinion, it would be ruinous to the popular cause to abandon. His efforts, ably seconded by Colonel Easton,[55] finally induced the leading patriots in Connecticut and Massachusetts to concur in the propriety of retaining the forts, and some of them supported his proposed invasion of Canada. Arnold, of course, opposed whatever Allen approved. He ridiculed Allen's proposed attack upon Montreal; and continued his exertions to send the cannon to Massachusetts. The Congress of that State, believing itself responsible for Arnold's acts, were constantly sending letters of excuse and apology for them to the Conti-

---

[53] Force, p. 693. [54] Force, p. 715.
[55] See Easton's letter to Prov. Con. of Mass. Force's Archives, 919.

nental Congress and their sister colonies.[56] But, while they were thus exerting themselves to excuse him, he did not hesitate to open communication for himself with all the sources of power. He was in frequent correspondence with the Continental, as well as the Congresses of Connecticut and New York, and, in the early part of June, it is difficult to determine to which of these bodies, if to either, he held himself responsible.

The Congress of Massachusetts was well informed of Arnold's movements, and, before the end of May, had become convinced of the necessity of asserting an absolute control over his lawless imprudence. To avoid doing him any injustice, they determined to examine into his conduct, and, in the meantime, not to excuse his further rashness, by any sudden withdrawal of their confidence. With this view they addressed him a letter on the 27th of May, assuring him that they would receive no impressions to his disadvantage, until they had given him an opportunity to vindicate his conduct;[57] and, on the same day, despatched Colonel Joseph Henshaw, to Hartford, with instructions, if Connecticut had made provision for garrisoning Ticonderoga, to proceed to that place, and order Arnold to return to Massachusetts, and settle his accounts and be discharged. Of this resolution the Congress advised Arnold in their letter of the same date. Upon reaching Hartford, Colonel Henshaw learned that Connecticut had already sent Colonel Hinman, with a well appointed force of a thousand men, to Ticonderoga, to take the command, and hold the place until New York was prepared to relieve them. Colonel Henshaw, instead of proceeding to Ticonderoga himself, despatched a letter by special express to Arnold, informing him of Colonel Hinman's departure, and that it was the expectation of the Massachusetts Congress that he should assume the command upon his arrival, and, to leave no question of authority open,

---

[56] See Letter of Mass. Cong. to Conn. Force, 722. [57] Force, 723.

and no excuse for Arnold's attempting to retain the command, the Massachusetts Committee of Safety, which had originally commissond Arnold, *without the knowledge of the Congress*, on the 28th of May, wrote him that the Congress had now taken up the matter, and given the necessary orders respecting the acquisition of these forts. As if in anticipation of Arnold's disobedience, the letter adds, "it *becomes your duty, and is our requirement*, that you conform yourself to such advice and orders as you shall, from time to time, receive from that body." [58]

Arnold had no intention of surrendering his authority, although directed to do so, both by Connecticut and Massachusetts. As soon as he received information of Colonel Hinman's approach, he became "positive" that an invasion of Canada ought to be attempted, and that he could easily take Montreal and Quebec. He, therefore, proposed to the Continental Congress that, "to give satisfaction to the different colonies," Colonel Hinman's regiment should form part of an army of two thousand men, which, under his command, should invade the Canadian Provinces. He expressed the emphatic wish that this army should include "*no Green Mountain Boys!*" This letter he despatched to Philadelphia by one of his captains, as a special express.

Just at this time the colonies, while opposed to the invasion of Canada, had become fully awakened to the vital importance of holding Ticonderoga at all hazards. A full month had elapsed after the capture before they became aware of the value, in a military sense, of the position, which was clear to Allen before its seizure was attempted. The feeling of the leading patriots on the subject is well expressed in a letter to General Warren, written from Northampton by Joseph Hawley, on the 9th of June.[59] Speaking of Ticonderoga, he says: "I am still in

---

[58] Force, 723-727.   [59] Force, 944.

agonies for the greatest possible despatch to secure that pass." He points out that it is the spot where the greatest mischief to the colonies "may be withstood and resisted; but, if that is relinquished or taken from us, desolation must come in upon us like a flood." "The design of seizing that fort was gloriously conceived; but to what purpose did our forces light there, if they are now to fly away?" In these and like emphatic terms, he urged that Ticonderoga should be strengthened without the loss of a day. Its importance was beginning to be understood; none knew it better than Arnold, and the idea of losing its command at such a time was resisted by all the selfish impulses of his soul.

The report of Colonel Henshaw to the Massachusetts Congress, early in June, had shown to that body the propriety of allowing Connecticut to appoint the commander-in-chief of Ticonderoga, and the necessity of settling all questions of precedence, so far as Arnold was concerned. His purpose to resist his own removal had already been foreshadowed, though it was not believed he would proceed to the extremity of actual mutiny. There was evidence enough, however, to induce that Congress to inform itself thoroughly of the condition of affairs upon this frontier. It had already called upon its Committee of Safety for copies of Arnold's commission; the papers relating to his appointment; the engagements of the Committee to him; the authority they had conferred upon him, and "everything necessary to give the Congress a full understanding of the relation Colonel Arnold then stood in to the Colony." [60] On the 12th of June, it resolved to appoint three persons to repair to Ticonderoga, examine into the state of affairs there, and act in such a manner as the Congress should direct. The importance of this action, in the opinion of the Congress, is shown by the fact that the committee, which con-

[60] Force, 716.

sisted of Walter Spooner, Jedediah Foster and James Sullivan, were elected by ballot, and another committee was appointed to prepare their instructions. These instructions were presented to the Congress, and approved on the 13th, and given to the committee on the 14th of June. They were minute and specific, and covered the whole subject. They directed the committee to retain Arnold in the service *only* in case he was willing to serve at one or both of the posts, under the command of such chief officer as Connecticut might appoint, and, in that event, they were to continue him in commission, if they should judge it best " for the general service and safety," after having made themselves " fully acquainted with the spirit, capacity and conduct of said Arnold." They were fully empowered to discharge him, and, in that event, were to direct him to return to the colony and settle his accounts. They were also directed to inform themselves thoroughly of the past transactions in this quarter, and with every fact which would enable them to advise the Congress intelligently; and to act for the common interest of the colonies.[61]

These instructions invested the committee with all the powers which the Congress itself could have exercised, and they were limited in their action only, by their own discretion. The committee immediately departed upon their mission, the history of which is given in their report on the 6th of the following July, and the various letters written by themselves and others in the intervening period.

Upon reaching Ticonderoga, the committee found a remarkable condition of affairs. Colonel Hinman, with his regiment, had arrived; but, instead of turning over the command, Arnold had transferred it to Captain Herrick, from whom Colonel Hinman's men were obliged to take their orders, or were not suffered to pass to and from the garrison. The committee

---

[61] See Proc. Prov. Con. of Mass., June 13, 1775.

entered upon their investigations, determined to inform themselves of all the facts before taking any active measures. Their report sheds light upon the capture, and confirms the correctness of Allen's account. This report ought to be accepted as full proof of the facts it contains, for it comprises the conclusions of an impartial committee of the body under which Arnold claimed to have acted, made upon a thorough examination of the facts, within a month after the events transpired. The committee had copies of Arnold's commission and instructions. They state that they " informed themselves, as fully as they were able, in what manner he had executed his said commission and instructions, and find that he was with Colonel Allen and others at the time the fort was reduced, *but do not find that he had any men under his command at the time of the reduction of these fortresses!*" After the lapse of nearly a hundred years, can Arnold's admirers hope successfully to contradict this *quasi* judicial determination of the question which the committee had undertaken to set at rest forever![62]

Some of the experiences of the committee it would have been indiscreet further to publish to the enemy, and they must be sought elsewhere than in their report. But the facts were recorded at the time by men of unimpeachable veracity. The report states that Arnold did possess himself of the sloop on the lake, at St. Johns, and that the committee found him " claiming the command of said sloop and a schooner, which is said to be the property of Major Skene; and also all the posts and fortresses at the south end of Lake Champlain and Lake George, although Colonel Hinman was at Ticonderoga, with near a thousand men under his command at the several posts."

Arnold was at Crown Point, some twelve miles from Ticonderoga, when the committee arrived; and, without interfering

---

[62]See Report of this Committee. Force, 1596.

with affairs at the latter place, the committee passed on to the former, where the vessels were. Arnold was prepared for their reception, and had sent a strong force on board the vessels. The committee informed him of their commission, and, at his request, gave him a copy of their instructions, upon reading which, "he seemed greatly disconcerted." His conclusion was no sudden outburst of anger. It was taken "after some time contemplating upon the matter;" and after the committee had informed him, in writing, that it was the expectation of the Congress of Massachusetts, that the officer in command of the Continental forces should command the posts, and that the committee required him to conform to the instructions of the Congress, and deliver the command to the proper Connecticut officer. He then peremptorily refused to comply with the instructions, and declared that "he would not be second in command to any person whomsoever." It is unimportant whether the committee thereupon discharged him from the service, as stated by Mott, or he resigned his commission in the impudent letter of June 24th, which he sent to the committee.[63]

The result was a mutiny! for which Arnold was responsible as the chief instigator. According to Mott's statement, the committee desired the privilege of speaking with Arnold's men, but were not permitted to do so. Arnold and a portion of his men retired on board the vessels, and threatened to sail to St. Johns and deliver themselves up to the enemy. He states that Arnold had disbanded all the men but those on board the vessels, which had drawn off into the lake; that the committee left the post in a state of anarchy; that they were threatened and ill-treated while there, and when they came away, *were actually fired upon with swivels and small arms by Arnold's people.*

---

[63] See App., No. 25.

Mott thereupon obtained permission from Colonel Hinman to proceed from Ticonderoga to Crown Point, and, if possible, board the vessels. He was accompanied by Colonel Sullivan, a member of the committee, Lieutenant Halsey, and a Mr. Duer, one of the civil appointees of New York, for the county of Charlotte, who was very influential in composing the difficulty. They got on board the vessels about eleven o'clock the next morning. Arnold separated the party, placing some of the members on each vessel, under guards with fixed bayonets, and so kept them until evening, when they were permitted to return. They found opportunities, however, to converse with the men, and convinced some of them of their error, who declared that they had been deceived by Arnold. Colonel Sullivan was grossly insulted while on board the vessels, especially by Brown, one of Arnold's captains. The party returned to Ticonderoga, whence Colonel Hinman sent a detachment back to Crown Point, which succeeded, the next day, in gaining possession of the vessels.

On the 24th, Arnold made a written resignation of his commission, and the committee, with the aid of Colonel Hinman, John Brown, Surgeon Jonas Fay, and others, succeeded in restoring the order and discipline of the two posts, and in arranging all the difficulties with the men. Their judicious conduct rescued the country from a peril almost as fearful as that in which Arnold afterwards involved it on the banks of the Hudson. It seems almost inconceivable how any officer of the Revolutionary army could have trusted Arnold after this conclusive proof of his utter selfishness and want of patriotism. Had he carried out his threat of delivering up the vessels, and with them the command of the lake to the enemy, the consequences must have been disastrous, if not fatal, to the cause of popular liberty.[94]

---

[94] Force, 1591, 96.

Returning now to Arnold's own account of affairs in this vicinity, which has been somewhat anticipated in giving a connected relation of the action of Massachusetts in the premises, we find his next letter dated on the 23d of May, at Crown Point, and directed to the Massachusetts Committee of Safety.[65] It is unimportant, except for its ungenerous remarks upon the failure of Allen's attempt upon St. Johns. On the 26th, he advises the same committee of his purpose to send some of the captured guns to Massachusetts as soon as possible. It is in his letter of May 29th, to the Continental Congress, that he undertakes to give the second version of his participation in the command at the time of the capture.[66]

Arnold could never tell the story of his command twice alike. Three weeks before, he had written, "*I had agreed with Colonel Allen* to issue further orders jointly." Now he says, that near the fort, he "met one Colonel Allen, with about one hundred men, raised at the instance of *some gentlemen from Connecticut, who agreed* that we should take a joint command." He adds, "some dispute arising between Colonel Allen and myself, prevented my carrying my orders into execution." The "gentlemen from Connecticut" have recorded their emphatic contradiction of the statements of this letter.

The third and concluding version of the joint command, although nominally the work of a third person, bears strong evidence that it was inspired by Arnold himself, the confessed author of the two others. In Thomas' "Oracle of Liberty," of May 24th, an account of the capture, given by Colonel Easton, had been published, which assigned the command to Allen, gave Easton a conspicuous position in the seizure, but made no mention of Arnold. It was contradicted in Holt's "New York Journal," of June 25th, by a writer under the pseudonym of "Veritas," who professed to have been one of

---

[65] Force, 693.   Force, 734.

the attacking party, and an eye-witness of the capture. According to "Veritas," the Connecticut Committee were joined by Easton, *after their arrival upon the Grants*, though it is well known that Easton came with the committee from Pittsfield. He states that Arnold, having concerted a similar plan, "proceeded to the party under the command of Colonel Allen," and that "when Colonel Arnold made known his commission, etc., *it was voted by the officers present* that he should take a joint command with Colonel Allen (Colonel Easton not presuming to take any command)." According to *Veritas*, the Green Mountain Boys were very unwilling to cross the lake; but "Colonel Arnold, with much difficulty, persuaded about forty" of them to do so! When they got over, these still wished to await the arrival of the rest of the party, but "Arnold urged to storm the fort immediately, declaring he would enter it alone if no man had courage enough to follow him!" He says that Arnold was the first to enter the fort, Allen being about five yards behind him; that Arnold demanded the surrender—Easton being hid away in an old barrack, under pretence of drying his gun. He also relates that he had the pleasure of seeing Easton heartily kicked by Arnold," etc.

Arnold has now exhausted all the sources from which his joint command could be derived, save one. First, he has it by an agreement with Allen himself; next, by an agreement with the Connecticut Committee, and, thirdly, by a vote of the officers present. Had he given a fourth account, he would probably have secured it from the vote of the men, who proposed to disband upon the suggestion that they were to be placed under his authority.

The remarkable effusion of "Veritas" is followed in Force's Archives[87] by three documents, which clearly evince the same paternity. One of them, directed to "The Printer," refers to

---

[87] Force, 1085, 90.

an address "from the inhabitants on Lake Champlain, *to the worthy Colonel Arnold*, who, on the first alarm of the ravage and bloodshed committed by the Ministerial troops at Lexington, marched with his company of cadets, from New Haven, to the assistance of his bleeding countrymen." It states that on the march he concerted the plan for the reduction of Ticonderoga and Crown Point, and the Provincial Congress and Committee of Safety approving of his plan, and confiding in his judgment and fidelity, commissioned him to reduce the same, which, "by his vigilence and prudence he soon effected;" that, without the loss of one man, he obtained the command of an extent of country one hundred and sixty miles in length, which cost the British nation two millions of money and two campaigns," etc., etc. The writer consoles himself for the loss of a Warren, and many other worthy men, by the reflection that *an Arnold is yet preserved*, "who, though enemies misrepresent his conduct, will yet be found to merit the highest approbation."

The address to Arnold is still more fulsome and adulatory. It purports to have been signed by the principal inhabitants on the lake, in behalf of themselves and six hundred families contiguous thereto, who, deeply impressed with a sense of his merit, and their weighty obligations to him, testify their gratitude and thankfulness for his important conquests, his benevolence to the inhabitants, his tenderness to the prisoners, his humane and polite manner, which have shown a bright example "of that elevation and generosity of soul, which nothing less than real magnaminity and *innate virtue* could inspire." After a column of this material, they conclude by expressing their sorrow for his approaching removal, and lamenting their situation at the thoughts of losing him. The receipt of this document is acknowledged by a note from Arnold, printed in the same connection.

There can be no necessity for wasting time in the refutation of these documents addressed to, or concerning, a man who at that date was actually engaged in corrupting his men, and creating a mutiny. That Arnold supervised, if he did not dictate them, is as certain as if they appeared over his own signature. Of course the address is not signed; the name is not given of one of the principal inhabitants, or six hundred families. There were not that number within ten miles of Lake Champlain, and the few settlers along the lake held Arnold in detestation. Who but Arnold, or his valet, could have given that minute account of his actions, and even his thoughts, all the way from Cambridge to Castleton? Who but he, in the assaulting party, would have written such an account? Such trash is only valuable to enable us to form an estimate of the man—proud, arrogant, selfish, and so conceited that he thought all the world admired him. These documents proclaim their authorship, and refute themselves. They are contradicted by every witness, every known fact, and every circumstance in every important particular.

The advocates of Arnold seek to strengthen their case by asserting that he remained here in command after Allen had withdrawn, and his party had returned to their homes. My limits will not allow me to pursue the history into further details. I leave the subject with this statement: Arnold was never in command of Ticonderoga during this campaign. Immediately after the capture, he left Ticonderoga, where he was hated by the men, and an annoyance to the officers, and went to Crown Point, where Allen and Warner were content that he should exercise his brief authority. Whatever he did, was done there, and there the Massachusetts Committee found him, when they finally dismissed him from the service.

Benedict Arnold possessed few of the qualities of which heroes are made. The native generosity of his countrymen has induced them to give him more credit than he ever deserved for his service in the cause of popular liberty, and has led some of them to attempt excuses for his crimes. He has even been represented as the victim of misfortune, slowly driven to treason by the consciousness of unrequited merit, and the conviction that inferior men were preferred before him. The effort to make him the hero of Ticonderoga is of recent origin, and was never undertaken while the witnesses were living, and their evidence fresh in the public mind. The desire of the American people not to deal unjustly with a great criminal has given it some currency. The facts of his life, when thorougly comprehended, assign him his true place in history—among the most dangerous of unprincipled men. They disclose a character in which selfishness was the controlling element. It gave impulse to every thought of his mind; it directed every action of his body. It was displayed in the precocity of a wicked childhood; even then he was wayward and vicious, seeking his keenest pleasures in the torture and destruction of dumb, defenseless animals. As he grew older, his corrupted tastes and evil habits destroyed the happiness of an excellent mother; and an attempt to murder, while yet a boy, sufficed to cloud a sister's whole life with sorrow. The son of an obscure sea-faring man, he varied the monotony of his youthful experiences by voyages to the West Indies, horse trading in Canada, fighting a duel, and enlistments in and desertions from the service. Such activity in evil courses indicated ability, if he could be subjected to restraint, and friends were found who furnished capital to establish him in business, in the hope that he would settle down and abandon his wicked ways. The news of Lexington found him a small druggist, and the captain of a volunteer company in New Haven. Love of excitement, and a passion for destructiveness, more than any motive of patriotism, led him to join the army. How he came to this frontier we have already seen. Here, he claimed that his early experiences had given him a knowledge of naval affairs; and, with the schooner which Herrick had captured from Major Skene, and some smaller craft, he fitted out a little fleet, and with it took the British vessels on the lake. Of that force he was the real commander, and of none other. His teeming brain daily gave birth to some rash and dangerous project, by which his own advancement was to be promoted. He divided men into two parties,—his friends, who admired his greatness, and his enemies, who were envious of his fame, and were constantly engaged in efforts to undermine and destroy him. He secured his commission, confident that it would give him the chief command in this quarter, and his failure to secure it filled him with angry disappointment. He was unpopular with the soldiers, feared by his inferiors, despised by all. We have seen how his rashness involved the colonies in serious difficulties, and how prudently Massachusetts undertook to control him, and make him useful to the country, while he was impressing all who knew him with what Captain Mott calls "his extraordinary ill conduct." Impatient under investigation, maddened that his authority should be questioned, unable to dispose of Colonel Hinman, he was ready, when the Massachusetts Committee reached Ticonderoga, to scout their authority and defy their power. When peremptorily ordered to turn over his command, this model patriot and military leader, with such of his men as he could control, broke into open mutiny, retired on board the vessels, and threatened to desert and deliver them up to the enemy. He even attempted the lives of the committee, after he had subjected them to threats and imprisonment. Finally, having quarrelled with his brother officers, abandoned by his soldiers, unable longer to resist the committee, powerless for further evil, in disgrace with everybody, he flung up his commission and vanished from the scene. The war presented no parallel instance of treasonable insubordination. Was it strange that Colonel Brown, in the next campaign, and years before his greater crime, posted him as a robber of prisoners, who surrendered on the faith of his promises; a murderer of defenseless non-combatants, and a traitor ready made when his price was tendered! that he should marry a Tory heiress, and enter upon a life of extravagant debauchery, which could only be supported by fraud and peculation upon the public treasury; that he was convicted by a court martial, and reprimanded by Washington! that his treason culminated at the first favorable opportunity; and, finally, that his murderous ravages in his native and other States, should have shown that all the accidents of all the wars on this continent never brought to the surface of public life any man so thoroughly depraved as he whose name has become a synonym for the highest treason! True, he fought well at Stillwater, but at that moment he was devising plans for revenge upon his associates for fancied slights, and plotting new schemes to relieve himself from the debts in which his courses had involved him. A few acts of bravery, a few spasms of patriotism, scattered like fitful gleams through the darkness of a wicked life, instead of excusing his treachery, only serve to make it more conspicuous. It is time to have done with apologies for the worst man ever born on American soil; with efforts to excite the world's admiration for a man who possibly might have been a patriot, if he had not been a traitor. It is time to strip from his deformity the mantle which a mistaken charity has thrown over it. In the world's history there have been two conspicuous traitors. But there is a choice between them, and one was the better man,—for he repented of his treason, cried out that he had shed innocent blood, threw down his thirty pieces, and went and hanged himself! The other wasted his price upon his vices, was pensioned by his purchasers, and went detested and unrepentant to his foreign grave! He was a bad boy and a worse man, depraved and unprincipled from his cradle to his latest day. His claims to the respect of true men are just as good, when he is selling his country on the banks of the Hudson, as when he is writing false letters from the shores of Lake Champlain.

It is neither my desire nor my purpose to defend Ethan Allen. I am not here to set forth his virtues, or apologise for his faults. That there were grave defects in his character is neither denied nor sought to be concealed. His generous, impulsive nature; his complete self-confidence, which led him to believe himself equal to any enterprise; his intense hatred for tyranny and oppression in all their forms, were qualities which do not exist in man, except in connection with strong passions, and other objectionable elements. He belonged to a class who are most popular with those who know them best, and are usually misjudged by those who know little of them. For he was careless of the opinions of others, and seemed to delight in misleading them in their judgment of himself. He despised the acts by which popularity is courted; and those who count him a demagogue may be defied to point to a single word he ever uttered, a single act he ever performed, merely to gain the popular applause. He was of large stature and strong muscle, capable of great exertion and endurance, and he feared nothing under the sun. His education was better than that of the average of men in those days, when but little time could be spared for instruction, in the severe and universal struggle for existence. With proper training, he would have been capable of intellectual eminence, for he has left many evidences that he was able to seize and present effectually the points in an argument. Falsehood and tergiversation were so offensive to him, that he would not tolerate them even to promote his own interests, and he detested injustice of every description with all the energy of his intense organization. Love of liberty was the controlling passion of his soul, inspiring every impulse, directing every action. In the presence of sorrow, he was gentle as a woman, and among the many traditions concerning him which have been preserved, those are most numerous which show his effective service in behalf of the poor, the unfortunate and the distressed. If his faults were grave, who has the right to say that they were not counterbalanced by his virtues?

But it is Allen's conduct during the campaign of 1775 that we are now considering, and in that, while there is much to praise, there is little to censure. Called out for a special purpose, on a moment's warning, with no preparation for a long service, when their work was done, Allen and his men expected to return to their homes. They remained here, performing all their duties as long as they were needed, and until they were properly relieved. Allen constantly reported to his superiors, and faithfully obeyed their orders. When Colonel Hinman reached Ticonderoga with his regiment, he was received cordially by Allen, who promptly turned over his command. Convinced that the Revolution had need of the Green Mountain Boys, Allen and Warner then hurried to Philadelphia, and asked from the Continental Congress authority to form them into a regiment. "I ask the privilege," Allen had already written, " of raising a small regiment of Rangers. It is, truly, the first favor I ever asked of the government; if it be granted, I will zealously endeavor to conduct myself for the best good of my country." In the presence of that august body, face to face with his old enemy, Duane, he told the story of Ticonderoga, and again presented his petition. The leader of a people claimed to be in rebellion, opened the doors of the Congress by his manly appeal. That body resolved to pay the Vermonters for their service here, and granted authority to raise a regiment, conditioned upon the approval of New York. With the resolution in his hands, authenticated by the signature of John Hancock, he returned to New York city, where the Provincial Congress was in session. There, was exhibited a scene which illustrates the patriotism of the time. To that Congress, whose authority he had so many times defied, and to whose constituents he had applied the "beech seal," he proposed to bury the old bitter feud beneath the wave of liberty then sweeping over the land. In vain the speculators in Vermont lands, and their agents, protested. In vain they exclaimed that he was "a felon, an outlaw with a price upon his head, and that it would disgrace the Congress to admit him within their doors!" "I move that Ethan Allen be permitted to have an audience at this board!" exclaims a member. "I second the motion!" shouts Smith, of Duchess, and by a vote of two to one, it was (says the record) "ordered that Ethan Allen be admitted." And the record continues, "Seth Warner was admitted at the same time." [66] What Allen said, we do not know; but we do know that the envoys from the mountains were heard, and that, at the same setting, the Congress, which a year before had proclaimed Allen a traitor, and offered a reward to any who would hunt him down, confirmed the order of the Continental Congress, and sent Allen to General Schuyler, with authority to raise the regiment, which should elect its own officers, and with directions which secured Schuyler's co-operation. It did no great harm that "the County of Albany" (the headquarters of the speculators) "and Mr. John DeLancey dissented to the above order and resolve."

The regiment was raised. Then occurred another event which brought out the qualities of Allen's character. Remember, he had been the military leader of the Grants from the beginning; his energy had overcome all the obstacles, and he had

[66] Force, 1338.

procured authority to raise the regiment—he should have been its colonel. Now, when the election of officers was made, the older settlers, distrusting his bold impetuosity, ignored his claims, and chose the more cautious Warner in his place. It was a cold and cruel neglect, for which there was no excuse. He might well be pardoned for having expressed his natural indignation. Did he resent the neglect, and, like Arnold, threaten desertion to the enemy? No! He scarcely uttered a word of complaint. He knew there was a place for him in the Revolution—if not as an officer, then as a private. "I hope the Congress will remember me," he wrote, "for I desire to remain in the service," and with all the energy of his soul he went into the contest. He fought his country's battles, and in her behalf endured, without a murmur, long years of insult and imprisonment. His sacrifices and sufferings every Vermonter knows. It does not surprise them that, three years later, the Father of his Country said of him: "His firmness and fortitude seem to have placed him out of the reach of misfortune. There is something about him that *commands* our admiration." There was a place for him in the Revolution—there is a place for him in history. He needs no monument to perpetuate his fame. As the wheels of time roll on, a grateful country forgets his faults, and remembers him for his daring courage, his generous heart, his fidelity to his country, and his unselfish devotion to the State he loved. Compare such a man with Benedict Arnold! The soldier of freedom with the soldier of fortune! Hercules to Cacus! Hyperion to a Satyr! "A beast, that wants discourse of reason," knows which is the hero and which the fraud.

I am aware that criticisms have been made upon the language in which Allen asserts that the demand for surrender was made. For example, it is said that he could not have made the reference to the Continental Congress, because that body was not in session until several hours after the surrender. These are too puerile to deserve notice. They never raised a doubt that the language was used, save in the minds of the very limited number of persons no better informed than the authors of these suggestions.

The subsequent history of Ticonderoga has many points of interest. The command of Schuyler; the return here, in 1776, of the remnants of Montgomery's shattered army, saved by the energy of the Vermonters, turning out in answer to Wooster's call; the coming of Gates,—his summons to the Green Mountain militia, who were publicly thanked by him for defending yonder fort from capture; their gathering here again in 1777, under Warner and St. Clair,—the retreat of the latter, the stubborn, gallant fight at Hubbardton; Bennington and Saratoga; the ravages of the British in 1778—their invasion in 1780, when they scoured the country as far down as Stillwater; the negotiations with Canada, in 1781, which have given so much distress to the enemies of Vermont; the appearance of the British here in force, in October of that year, when the Vermonters "put the hook in their nose, and turned them back by the way whence they came," with others, enough to fill a volume, must be wholly omitted. Many of them have been recorded in that best of "Early Histories," written by your venerable ex-President. They are incidents over which the children of Vermont will linger with interest through all coming time.

I have, thus, once more presented the history of the capture of Ticonderoga. I think I have referred to all the material evidence which bears upon the origin of the expedition, or the question of command. Right well I know that I have repeated an "oft told tale." The assaults of Allen's maligners; their claims in behalf of Arnold have been often exposed and refuted. But the leaven of old prejudices against Vermont and her early settlers is still active. There are those who, even now, cannot be comforted at the thought, that in spite of all their enemies, the Green Mountain Boys wrought out their independence,— who believe that a false charge acquires strength by repetition. There are few false charges in history which have been reiterated with such blind malice, such persistence in error, as those against Allen and the Vermonters. When once set in motion, the vitality of a falsehood in history is something surprising. You may refute it, but it will not stay refuted. You may beat it down to-day, to-morrow it is up again, as vigorous as ever. Nay! you may slay it as dead as the creature of a prehistoric age, smitten to its brain center by a thunderbolt of the Almighty, —buried below the rocks of the Laurentian epoch, and turned to stone by the chemistry of cosmic ages; and there shall be some "man with the muck rake," some delver in the ruins of the past, who will rob the tomb of its skeleton, and bring it forth into the light of day; and, while its shape offends the sight of all others, to him it will seem an angelic form, of ambrosial fragrance and seraphic beauty! Thus has it been with the falsehoods against Allen and his men. Three times they have been refuted by members of this society. The origin of the expedition has been demonstrated and minutely described by an accomplished scholar of the State whence it came;[68] the historians of our country, some of them honored sons of New York, are agreed in their conclusions; and yet these writers of the new school of history, without facts, go on repeating their libels as though they were made stronger by repetition. There was a time when they might have been excused by the superficial knowledge and bitter prejudices of their authors. But not now. Those, who now repeat them, know them to be untrue. How-

[68] App. 26.

ever slight their general knowledge of American history, they must be presumed to have read the evidence which has been republished in answer to their charges; their ignorance of which, in the preparation of such charges, was wholly inexcusable. The repetition of such statements, after the evidence has been produced, and they have been pointed to its depositories, therefore, can have neither excuse nor apology. But they are repeated in the journals, in magazine articles, in addresses, occasional speeches,—in every form which may attract the public attention. Even a recent guide book offers to the traveler historical information like this: That the action of the Connecticut Committee was inspired by the letter of John Brown, from Canada; that the command was exercised, and the capture made by Arnold *and* Allen,—placing the traitor first; that Romans was with the party at Castleton, when Mott's careful record shows that "he left at Bennington, and joined no more;" that "an arrangement was made by which Arnold and Allen were to hold *something like* a joint command." In this book, the story of "Veritas," "six hundred families included," is rehashed and presented as a delicious morsel of history; and, while Arnold is portrayed as the "restorer of harmony,"—the Bayard without reproach,—Allen is declared to be "a sort of Robin Hood," who "played the part of a swaggering brigand."

But the gem of this volume, is the modest conclusion of its author, that he leaves "*Allen less a hero than he found him!*" Poor, indeed, is the record which can be dimmed or diminished by such an assailant! And these statements are to be accepted as facts in "the new era," upon which, according to this reverend defamer, "the study of American history has now entered." For the welfare of his flock, it is to be hoped that he is a safer guide in the "narrow way" than he is in the history of Ticonderoga.

In view of all the facts, it may not have been an unprofitable use of our time to have spent an hour, here, upon the ground and theatre of these important events, in vindicating the truth of a familiar history. Here was the first substantial triumph in arms of American liberty,—the step in advance which made retreat dishonorable, reconciliation impracticable. Here was the first victory, which strengthened the brave and confirmed the wavering. After the morning of the 10th of May, 1775, there was no alternative between thirteen conquered colonies and an independent nation. This triumph was won by our forefathers. It is our duty to see that their honors are not stolen away. I have no hope that I have presented this subject in any clearer light than those who have preceded me. But none of them have attempted to bring all the facts together, and present the entire history in detail, in a connected form. This work I have endeavored to do. I believe I have referred to all the material evidence, or pointed out the places where it may be found. If any of it is new, it will delight me to have made such a contribution to the treasury of history. As I understand history, its chief value consists in pointing out the repositories of the facts of which it is made, that those who choose may examine them for themselves. On such facts, so far as our present subject is concerned, Vermont may trust her cause to the impartial judgment of the world. Let diligent students of our revolutionary history,—who have no prejudices to satisfy, no preconceived opinions to support, no passions to blind them, and no theories to maintain,—answer the question which I proposed, at the commencement of this address, for themselves. Let them say whether it must not be answered now, as every honest historian has answered it for ninety-seven years ? *" Ticonderoga was captured by the Green Mountain Boys, led by Ethan Allen !"*

I hoped, on this occasion, to have briefly referred to that single other charge which the assailants of Vermont have attempted to establish upon the facts of her early record,—that of infidelity to the cause of the country, in the negotiations with Haldimand, in 1780-81. This charge was made at the time, and refuted, somewhat contemptuously by those whose integrity in this transaction was questioned; and it has been refuted as often as it has been renewed. There is a considerable amount of evidence on this subject, which has not recently been made public. In connection with facts already known, it not only excludes from that transaction any taint of suspicion, but shows it to have been a work of statesmanship, which not only protected Vermont in the most critical period of her existence, when threatened by powerful invasions, and by dangers which might have overwhelmed any State,—every soldier and gun of the national forces were withdrawn from her territory, and she was left to defend herself by her own resources,—but which powerfully contributed to the success of the national cause. Had time permitted, I should have laid some of this evidence before you. But it matters little; Vermont can afford to wait. The evidence will be preserved, and, if I do not, some other Vermonter will make it public. And then the world will know that no State in the Union had such a struggle for existence as ours; and that, in the whole twenty years of her stormy battle for life, there is no important fact or incident to be regretted by her children. Her early history will stand, in completeness and in detail, more interesting, dramatic and creditable to her pioneers, than that of any of her sisters. She entered upon her twenty years war, defended by a few courageous men. She carried it on against the forces of nature, surrounded by enemies, threatening her on every side. But her enemies never invaded her soil, unless to their own destruction.

She came out of the contest, not only the victor, but respected by all her sister States. With her honor untarnished, she took her seat as an equal at the National council board, where her voice has ever since been powerful on the side of freedom and justice; where it has never been raised in behalf of oppression or wrong. Her sons would be recreant descendants of her early soldiers and statesmen, if they did not guard her honor as their most precious inheritance.

Nor should the acts or words of individuals be charged against any of her sister States. Vermont has no controversy with New York—she never had. On the contrary, she is proud of the Empire State, and rejoices in her rapid march toward the commercial supremacy of the world. To suppose that the State of New York ever sought to swallow up Vermont, is to misunderstand the facts of history. There were "Rings," a hundred years ago, as powerful and selfish as those of to-day. One of them, composing high State officials, land jobbers and speculators, before the Revolution, for a time controlled the legislative and executive powers of that State, as effectively as others have controlled them at a recent period. They parcelled out the favors of royalty, and the lands of honest owners, to their favorites, but they never had the support or sympathy of the *people* of New York. The proof meets us at every turn. They proclaimed rewards, large and tempting in those days, for the capture of Ethan Allen. He went fearlessly to Albany, and no man molested him. They never could enforce their disgraceful laws, and never tried to enforce them. Their processes failed of service, for the "power of the county" would never come forth at their call. Their few attempts at arrest more nearly resembled kidnapping expeditions, than the ordinary execution of legal warrants. The instincts of a people are almost always on the side of justice. Those of the people of New York were always with the Vermonters. Later, her statesmen took up the contest in favor of Vermont, and stayed the hands of the speculators. Her historians have faithfully recorded the heroism of the Green Mountain Boys. There is no enmity between the two peoples, no jealousy between the two States. Nowhere have the false charges of the speculators of 1770, and the calumnies of a few of their descendants a century later, been visited with severer condemnation than among the intelligent historians, the distinguished statesmen, and the honest people of that great State, upon whose soil you have met to-day.

Fellow Citizens, Friends, Brother Vermonters! my work, here, is done. Would that it were better done; but, such as it is, I lay it on the altar of our history. It has, indeed, been a pleasant task for me. A Vermonter never knows how well he loves the Mountain State, until he has wandered beyond her borders, and lived among other surroundings. Then, every acre of her rugged soil, every leaf of her history, becomes dear to him. Then, he is as prompt in her defense against all assailants, as any true-hearted son to defend a beloved mother. I could not be otherwise than loyal to her! In the shadow of yonder mountains, four generations of my family have lived. There my children were born, and there I hope to rest, when the toils of this life are closed forever. Glorious Vermont! with thy life-giving air, thy grand old mountains, fertile valleys, laughing brooks, and lakes of silver! There is no fact of thy history which is not precious in the hearts of they children,—no blot on thy fair fame for them to remove! Grander and more glorious than the wealth of Crœsus, or the power of the Cæsars, is the heritage of thy people! What shall outvalue it? for what earthly treasure shall it be exchanged? Which of its elements shall be parted with, or cast aside? Behold, Vermonters, the wealth of your possessions! The example and influence of those early pioneers; a long line of honored statesmen, unbroken from the days of the "Grand Committee" to the present hour; the memories of Ticonderoga, Hubbardton and Bennington; your soldiers, first at every call, in the front on every field; rolling back the tide of invasion at Saratoga and Plattsburgh,—charging the heights of Chepultepec, unlocking the gates of victory at Gettysburg, gaining a lost battle at Cedar Creek, and aiding in the final crush of Rebellion on the banks of the Appomattox; your judiciary, never tarnished by the breath of suspicion; your legislature, incorruptible for an hundred years; your municipal organizations, town, city and county, never yet dishonored by a "ring;" your colleges and common schools, free to all, of every class, condition or color; your churches in every hamlet; your benevolent institutions, covering the poor at home, and stretching forth their protecting arms to the farthest islands of the sea; your thousand homes of comfort and plenty, cheered by affection and warmed by love; a prudent, plain and vigorous race of men; well trained, happy children; glorious, true hearted women. A better government, a happier people, will be sought in vain, within the limits of enlightened civilization. Such, Vermonters, is your inheritance, earned by the sacrifices and the blood of the men we honor to-day. For it all,—for her past history and present example; for all that Vermont has been, and is, and promises to be, you are largely their debtors. Teach, then, your children to keep their memories always green; and from the depths of the reverent, grateful hearts of every son and daughter of the State we love, let my closing prayer ascend to Heaven: "Vermont! God bless her! God bless her!"

APPENDIX.

APPENDIX.

NUMBER I. *Page* 14.

The reference, in the text, to Montcalm's exertions for the protection of the English, after the surrender of Fort William Henry, seems to be sustained by a fair balance of cotemporary evidence; and is confirmed by what is learned from other sources, of the character of the French commander. But it cannot be denied, that a portion of the evidence bears heavily against Montcalm, and indicates that he made little exertion to prevent the butchery. A specimen of this description of proof may be found in the graphic account of the massacre given by Captain Carver, who was one of the few inmates of the fort who were fortunate enough to escape. He says: "That in consideration of the gallant defense the garrison had made, they were permitted to march out with all the honors of war; to be allowed covered wagons to transport their baggage to Fort Edward, and a guard to protect them from the fury of the savages." But he declares, that although suffered to retain their arms, they were deprived of every round of ammunition, and when the prisoners were drawn out, they found the column completely surrounded by the savages. They began by stripping the prisoners of their clothing, and slaughtering the sick and wounded. The war whoop was finally given, and the Indians began to murder those nearest to them, without distinction. Men, women and children were despatched in the most wanton and cruel manner, and immediately scalped. Many of the savages drank the blood of their victims, as it flowed from their wounds.

"We now," he continues, "perceived, though too late to avail us, that we were to expect no relief from the French; and that, contrary to the agreement they had so lately signed, to allow us a sufficient force to protect us from these insults, they tacitly permitted them, for I could plainly perceive the French officers walking about at some distance, discussing together, with apparent unconcern. For the honor of human nature, I would hope that this flagrant breach of every sacred law proceeded rather from the savage disposition of the Indians, which I acknowledge it is sometimes almost impossible to control, and which might now, unexpectedly, have arrived to a pitch not easily to be restrained, than to any premeditated design in the French commander. An unprejudiced observer would, however, be apt to conclude that a body of ten thousand Christian troops (*most Christian troops*) had it in their power to prevent the massacre from becoming so general." After a thrilling account of his own escape to Fort Edward, he concludes:

"It was computed that 1500 persons were killed or made prisoners by these savages during this fatal day. Many of the latter were carried off by them, and never returned. A few, through favorable accidents, found their way back to their native country, after having experienced a long and painful captivity."—*Carver's Travels in America*, Ed. 1778, pp. 316 *to* 325.

—An evidence of the existence of the war between the two great Indian nations, to which reference is made in the text, at the discovery of Canada, may, perhaps, be found in the following extract from the relation of Cartier's second voyage. It was upon this voyage, in the year 1535, that he ascended the St. Lawrence to Hochelaga, and gave the name "Mont Royale" to the mountain, at the foot of which is the present city of Montreal. From this mountain, looking southward, he was the first white man who beheld the Adirondacks and the Green Mountains. After his return, in boats, down the river, to the Island of Orleans, where his ships had been left, the "Lord of the Country" came to him, and desired him, the next day, "to come and see Canada, which he promised to doe."

"The next day, being the 13th of the month (October, 1535), he, with all his gentlemen, and fiftie mariners, very well appointed, went to visite *Donnacona* and his people, about a leaguo from our ships. The place where they make their abode is called Stadacona. When we were about a stone's cast from their houses, many of the inhabitants came to meet us, being all set in a ranke, and (as their custome is) the men all on one side, and the women on the other, still dancing and singing, without any ceasing; and, after we had saluted and received one another, our Captaine gave them knives, and such other sleight things; then he caused all the women and children to passe along before him, giving each one a ring of Tin, for which they gave him hearty thankes; that done, our Captaine was, by Donnacona and Taignoagny, brought to see their houses, which (the qualitie considered) were very well provided, and stored with such victuals as the countrey yieldeth, to passe away the winter withall. Then they shewed us the skins of five men's heads, spread upon boards, as we doe use parchments. Donnacona told us that they were skins of Toudamani, *a people dwelling toward the South, who continually doe warre against them*. Moreover, they told us that it was two yeares past that those Toudamans came to assault them, yea, even into the said river, in an island that lyeth over against Saguenay, where they had bin the night before, as they were going a warfaring in Hognedo, with 200 persons, men women and children, who beeing all asleepe in a fort that they had made, they were assaulted by the said Toudamans, who put fire round about the fort, and as they would have come out of it to save themselves, they were all slaine, only five excepted, who escaped. For which losse they yet sorrowed, shewing with signes that one day they would be revenged; that done, we came to our ships againe."—*Hakluyt's Voyages*, Vol. III., p. 223.

NUMBERS II., III. Page 25.

Peleg Sunderland was one of the most active and energetic of the early settlers of Vermont. John Brown says that he "was an old Indian hunter, acquainted with the St. Francois Indians and their language." His associate upon this journey was Winthrop Hoyt, who had been many years a captive among the Indians of the Caughnawaga tribe. Through the familiarity of his guides with the habits and language of the Indians, Mr. Brown was able to ascertain that the latter had already been urged to join the Royal forces against the people of Boston, and that they had refused to do so. Sunderland and Hoyt remained among them several days, and left them well disposed towards the New Englanders, whom they promised to join, if they took any part in the contest. The importance, especially to the people upon the northern portion of the Grants, of Brown's mission, was very great. The result of open war which they most dreaded, was an invasion of the Indians from Canada, through the instigation of the British. Their neutrality enabled all the settlers on the Winooski River to remove, with their effects, to the south-western portion of the Grants, and the Indians did not become active participants in the contest until the invasion of Burgoyne, in 1777.

Sunderland was compensated by the Legislature of Vermont for this service in 1787. From his petition, it appears that he was employed in it for twenty-nine days, and the committee, to which his petition was referred, reported that the service was proved to their satisfaction, and, upon their recommendation, he received for it "eight pounds fourteen shillings, in hard money orders." In Graham's Sketch of Vermont, p. 134, the following account is given of Sunderland's connection with the name of Onion River: "This river took its name from the following circumstance: A Mr. Peleg Sunderland, in 1761, in hunting for beaver on this stream, lost his way, and was nearly exhausted with fatigue and hunger, when a party of Indians fortunately met him, and, with great humanity, relieved his wants, and saved him from perishing. Their provisions were poor, but what they had they freely gave, and their kindness made amends for more costly fare. Their whole store consisted of *onions*, and Mr. Sunderland then gave to the stream, near which he was so providentially preserved, the name of *Onion* River, which it has ever since retained."

In resistance to the authority of New York, before the Revolution, Sunderland was one of the active leaders,—the most active, perhaps, after Allen, Warner and Baker. Of this, abundant evidence is furnished by the affidavits published in the fourth volume of the "Documentary History of New York," p. 864, *et seq.* One *Jacob Marsh*, gives a pathetic account of his experiences in Socialborough, in the year 1773. He declares that the Bennington mob had "taken off the roof from his house, split a number of boards, and done him other damage." That he had "been informed, and verily believes, that John Smith and Peleg Sunderland (both of Socialboro') were the captains or leaders of the mob;" and that "he verily believes, that if he should act in his office of Justice of the Peace, in the said county of Charlotte, his effects and property would be destroyed by said mob, and that his life would be in danger." He was furnished with a certificate, dated at Arlington, November 20, 1773, in these words: "These may sartify, that Jacob Marsh hath been examined and had on fare trial, so that our mob shall not medeal further with him, as long as he behaves." Benjamin Hough says that Sunderland was one of the party who "insisted that he should call together all the people of Durham, to their judgment seat,—that Allen declared that the day of judgment had come, when every man should be judged according to his works." Sunderland was one of the parties named in the celebrated proclamation, offering a reward for the capture of the leaders of the opposition to the New York authorities.

Sunderland appears to have been a captain of the Green Mountain Boys, during the Revolution. In 1782, a British officer having raised seventeen recruits in the county of Albany, undertook to conduct them through Vermont to Canada.

Passing through Arlington, they made prisoners of Lieutenant Blanchard and Seargent Ormsbee, whose father, Major Ormsbee, upon learning of his capture, and the route which the party had taken, after sending an express to inform Col. Ira Allen of the facts, directed *Captain Sunderland*, with a party of men, to pursue the enemy. The Captain took his hounds with him, who followed the enemy, by their scent, but did not overtake them before they had been captured by a party under Captain Eastman, of Rupert, which had been sent out by Allen, and waylaid them in a mountain pass. The hounds of Captain Sunderland followed the tracks to the very feet of the prisoners, thus showing that they were the same party who had been pursued from Arlington. They were brought before the Governor, examined, and committed to Bennington jail, from whence they were sent to Canada, and exchanged for Vermonters, who were prisoners of war.— *Allen's Hist. Vt., pp.* 230, 231.

The following is an extract from H. Hall's "*Early History of Vermont*," p. 471: "An examination of the records of Manchester, shows Captain Sunderland to have resided in that town until the year 1791; to have been the owner of real estate and other property, and to have possessed the confidence of his townsmen. In 1787, he was appointed at the head of a committee of three to draw instructions for the town representatives to the Assembly. On another occasion, he was one of a committee on the subject of the school lands of the town, and his name appears on the records on other important occasions. The date of his removal from Manchester, or the time and place of his death, has not been ascertained. He was evidently a man of intelligence, as well as of activity and enterprise, and of respectable standing in society."

It is stated by descendants of one of the families concerned, that Sunderland was one of the party who rescued the lost children of ELDAD TAYLOR, in 1780, an incident which forms the subject of one of D. P. Thompson's most interesting tales. It also exhibits the traits of character which made Ethan Allen so popular among his neighbors. The relation is thus given by Zadock Thompson, in his "Gazetteer of Vermont," in a note to his account of the town of SUNDERLAND:

"On the 31st of May, 1780, two daughters of Eldad Taylor, of Sunderland, Keziah, aged seven, and Betsey, aged four years, wandered into the woods. Not returning, the parents became alarmed, and commenced a search, which, with the aid of a few neighbors, was continued through the night, without success. The next day the search was continued by large numbers from this and the neighboring towns, until the middle of the afternoon of the third day, when it was relinquished, and the people who had been out collected together, with the view of returning to their homes. Among these was one who thought the search should not be abandoned, and this was ETHAN ALLEN. He mounted a stump, and soon all eyes were fixed upon him. In his laconic manner, he pointed to the father and mother of the lost children, now petrified with grief and despair, bade each individual present, and especially those who were parents, to make the case of these parents his own, and then say whether they could go contentedly to their homes, without making one further effort to save these dear little ones, who were probably now alive, but perishing with hunger, and spending their last strength in crying to father and mother to give them something to eat. As he spoke, his giant form was agitated, and the tears rolled down his cheeks, and, in the assembly of several hundred men, but few eyes were dry. "I'll go! I'll go!" was at length heard from every part of the crowd. They betook themselves to the woods, and before night the lost children were restored in safety to the arms of their distracted parents. It appeared that the first night they laid down at the foot of a large tree, and the second they spent upon a large rock. They obtained plenty of drink from the stream, but were very weak for want of food. They, however, both survived, and Betsey, the younger, is now (July, 1842) the wife of Captain John Munson, of Williston. The elder was the wife of John Jones, and died some years ago, in Williston."

NUMBER IV. Page 25.

The letter of John Brown to the Committee of Correspondence in Boston.

MONTREAL, March 29, 1775.

GENTLEMEN:—Immediately after the reception of your letters and pamphlets, I went to *Albany*, to find the state of the lakes, and established a correspondence with Dr. *Joseph Young*. I found the lakes impassable at that time. About a fortnight after, I set out for *Canada*, and arrived at *St. Johns* in fourteen days, having undergone almost inconceivable hardships,—the Lake *Champlain* being very high, the small streams and rivers, and great part of the country, for twenty miles each side of the lake, especially towards *Canada*, under water. The Lake *Champlain* was partly open, and partly covered with dangerous ice, which, breaking loose for miles in length, our crafts drove us against an island, and froze us in for two days, after which we were glad to foot it on land.

I delivered your letters to Messrs. *Thomas Walker* and *Blake*, and was very kindly received by the Committee of Correspondence at *Montreal*, from whom I received the following state of affairs in the Province of *Quebeck*. Governor *Carleton* is no great politician; a man of sour, morose temper; a strong friend to Administration, and the late Acts of the *British* Parliament, which respect *America*, particularly the *Quebeck* Bill; has restrained the liberty of the press, that nothing can be printed without examination and license. Application has been made to him for printing the address from the Continental Congress, and a refusal obtained. All the troops in this Province are ordered to hold themselves in readiness for *Boston* at the shortest notice. Four or five hundred snow-shoes are prepared, for what use they know not. Mr. *Walker* has wrote you, about three weeks since, and has been very explicit. He informs you that two regular officers (lieutenants) have gone off in disguise, supposed to be gone to *Boston*, and to make what discovery they can through the country.

I have the pleasure and satisfaction to inform you that, through the industry and exertions of our friends in *Canada*, our enemies are not, at present, able to raise ten men for Administration. The weapons that have been used by our friends to thwart the constant endeavors of the friends of Government (so-called), have been chiefly *in terrorem*. The *French* people are (as a body) extremely ignorant and bigoted, the curates or priests having almost the entire government of their temporal, as well as spiritual affairs. In *La Prairie*, a small village, about nine miles from Montreal, I gave my landlord a letter of address, and there being four *Cures* in the village, praying over the dead body of an old friar, the pamphlet was soon handed to them, who sent a messenger to purchase several of them. I made them a present of each of them one, and was desired to wait on them in the Nunnery, with the holy sisters. They appeared to have no disposition unfriendly toward the Colonies, but chose rather to stand neuter.

Two men from the *New Hampshire Grants* accompanied me over the Lakes. The one was an old *Indian* hunter, acquainted with the *St. Francis' Indians* and their language; the other was a captive many years among the *Caghnawaga Indians*, which is the principal of all the *Canadian Six Nations*, and western tribes of Indians, whom I sent to enquire and search out any intrigues carrying on among them. These men have this minute returned, and report that they were very kindly received by the *Caghnawaga Indians*, with whom they tarried several days. The *Indians* say they have been repeatedly applied to, and requested to oin with the King's Troops to fight *Boston*, but have peremptorily refused, and still intend to refuse. They are a very simple, politick people, and say that if they are obliged, for their own safety, to take up arms on either side, that they shall take part on the side of their brethren, the *English* in *New England*,—all the chiefs of the *Caghnawaga* tribe being of *English* extraction, captivated in their infancy. They have wrote a friendly letter to Colonel *Israel Putnam*, of *Pomfret*, in *Connecticut*, in consequence of a letter which Colonel *Putnam* sent them, in which letter they give their brother *Putnam* assurance of their peaceable disposition. Several *French* gentlemen of *Montreal* have paid the Governour a visit, and offered him their services, as officers, to raise a *Canadian* Army, and join the King's Troops. The Governour told them he could get officers in plenty, but the difficulty consisted in raising soldiers.

There is no prospect of Canada sending delegates to the Continental Congress. The difficulty consists in this: Should the *English* join in the Non-Importation Agreement, the *French* would immediately monopolize the *Indian* trade. The *French* in *Canada* are a set of people who know no other way of procuring wealth and honour, but by becoming Court sycophants; and, as the introduction of the French laws will make room for the *French* gentry, they are very thick about the Governor. You may depend that, should any movement be made among the French to join against the Colonies, your friends here will give the shortest notice possible; and the Indians, on their part, have engaged to do the same, so that you have no occasion to expect to be surprised without notice, should the worst event take place.

I have established a channel of correspondance through the *New Hampshire Grants*, which may be depended on. Mr. *Walker's* letter comes by the hand of Mr. *Jeffers*, once of *Boston*, now on his way thither, which, together with this, is a full account of affairs here. I shall tarry here some time, but shall not go to *Quebeck*, as there are a number of their Committee here.

One thing I must mention, to be kept a profound secret. The Fort at *Ticon-*

deroga must be seized as soon as possible, should hostilities be committed by the King's Troops. The people on *New Hampshire Grants* have engaged to do this business, and, in my opinion, they are the most proper persons for this job. This will effectually curb this Province, and all the troops that may be sent here.

As the messenger to carry this letter has been waiting some time, with impatience, I must conclude, by subscribing myself, gentlemen, your most obedient, humble servant,

JOHN BROWN.

To Mr. SAMUEL ADAMS, } Committee of Correspondance in Boston.
Dr. J WARREN,

I am this minute informed that *Mr. Carleton* has ordered that no wheat go out of the river, until further orders; the design is obvious.

NUMBER V. *Page* 28.

A Vindication of the Opposition of the Inhabitants of Vermont to the Government of New York, and of their Right to form into an Independant State. Humbly submitted to the Consideration of the Impartial World. By ETHAN ALLEN. Printed by Alden Spooner, 1779: Printer to the State of Vermont.

The following extract from this pamphlet precedes the portion of it which is cited in the text, commencing on the ninth page:

"The approaching rupture between *Great Britain* and the *Colonies* was matter of serious reflection to the inhabitants of this frontier; their controversy with New York having (at great expense) been previously submitted to the King and Privy Council, by the negotiation of special agents, at two different times, and was in a high probability of being determined in their favor, which influenced some of the inhabitants to take a part with *Great Britain;* the more so, as this part of the country was a frontier, and, of consequence, would be greatly under the enemy's power, who was then in possession of *Ticonderoga, Crown Point* and *St. Johns,* and commanded the Lake with a vessel of force, besides. At the same time, their settlements were extended on the east side of the Lake, almost to the Province of *Quebec.* This was their situation when on the very eve of a war with *Great Britain.*

The Battle of *Lexington* almost distracted them, for interest inclined them to favor the royal side of the dispute; but the stronger impulses of affection to their country excited them to resent its wrongs, and obtain satisfaction for the blood of their massacred countrymen. Their condition was truly perplexed and critical; their hopes were placed on the royal authority for their deliverance from the encroachments and oppressions of the Government of *New York;* but the ties of consanguinity, personal acquaintance and friendship, similarity of religion and manners to the *New England* Governments, from whom these inhabitants had most generally emigrated, weighed very heavy in their deliberations; besides, the cause of the country was generally believed to be just, and that resistance to *Great Britain* had become the indespensable duty of a free people. But there was one very knotty query, which exercised the minds of their best politicians, viz.: Provided they should take an active part with their country; and, furthermore, provided an accommodation should take place, and the Colonies return to their former allegiance, what would then become of them, or their remonstrances against the Government of *New York*, lodged at the Court of *Great Britain?* But this danger seems to have been luckily passed over.

Soon after the news of the *Lexington* Battle, the principal officers of the Green Mountain Boys, and other principal inhabitants, were convened at *Bennington*, and attempted to explore futurity, but it was found to be unfathomable; and the scenes which have since taken place, then appeared to be precarious and uncertain. However, it was imagined that, provided those inhabitants were loyal to their country, and the event of the war should prove favorable to *America*, and their struggles for liberty should bring about a revolution, instead of a rebellion; that, in this case, they should rid themselves of the grievous usurpation of the Government of *New York*, and be entitled and readily admitted to any privileges which could reasonably be expected on revolution principles, which undoubtedly will be the consequence (for it can hardly be doubted, that, provided the said inhabitants had exercised the same degree of loyalty to the King that they have to the country, they might have shared as great privileges from the royal favor as they now request of Congress, viz.: Provided the event of the war had proved as successful to *Britain* as it has to *America*.) And as every of the Colonies and plantations were then taking arms for the mutual security of their liberty, and it was equally just and incumbent on the inhabitants of the *New Hampshire* Grants to do the same; it was therefore resolved to take an active part with the country, and thereby annihilate the old quarrel with the Government of New York, by swallowing it up in the general conflict for liberty; at that time not apprehending the least danger (on the proviso of a revolution's taking place) that Congress would resolve them to belong to the Government of *New York*, or in any manner countenance their being deprived of their liberty, by subjecting them under the power of a government which they detest more than that of the British, which they have manfully assisted the United States to suppress."

NUMBER VI. Page 29.

COL. SAMUEL H. PARSONS TO JOSEPH TRUMBULL.

NEW LONDON, 2d June, 1775.

Dear Sir:—A small sketch of my history since I saw you at Oxford may give you some satisfaction, and open a little the state of mind some gentlemen have been in the whole of last moon.

When I left you, I proceeded to Hartford, where I arrived Thursday forenoon [April 27]. You remember I remarked to you, I was concerned for the defenseless state (as I supposed) of our camp, and the want of heavy cannon, to effect anything against the town. On my way to Hartford, I fell in with Capt. Arnold, who gave me an account of the state of Ticonderoga, and that a great number of brass cannon were there. On my arrival at Hartford, Col. Sam. Wyllys, Mr. Deane and myself first undertook and projected taking that fort, etc.; and, with the assistance of three other persons, procured money, men, etc., and sent out on this expedition, without any consultation with Assembly, or others. This I mention only for this reason, that 'tis matter of diversion to me to see the various competitors for the honor of concerting and carrying this matter into execution, contending so strenuously about a matter, in the execution of which all concerned justly deserve applause. But some cannot bear an equal, and none a superior; and all make representations at the expense of truth, to monopolize what ought to be divided; but more of this another time. I waited at Hartford till Saturday,—got my heating orders, and went home. The next week my company was filled, and I had orders to march to Boston, and the week following began our march, when, to my surprise, the Sunday following, heard the Commissary had stopped the companies at Norwich. The same day I sent to Hartford a memorandum respecting the state of the case. My messenger returned Thursday; nothing done. The same day I went up myself, and could get no answer till Saturday noon, when my orders to march were countermanded, and my regiment ordered back to New London till further orders, where I now am, as much chagrined as any person need be; but this is a pleasure to my good friends, who feel a hearty satisfaction in mortifying me. The renowned Col. W., *the ambassador*, is the first on the list of my friends. He, on Saturday, mov'd that the further consideration of the destination of the troops might be further laid over (to bed, I suppose) for consideration. This *great man* is the same unchanged person who, I believe, would, even now, gladly baffle all overtures for our salvation.

I am now destined to this state of imprisonment, from whence I shall never be delivered without your help, and the assistance of Generals Spencer and Putnam. If proper representations of the necessity of more men at Boston, was made to the Governor by my friends in camp, I am certain he will order my regiment to Boston, immediately after the Assembly rises, which, I suppose, was last night, or will be this day. I beg you will use your interest to deliver one from this evil state as soon as possible.

What's become of our friend, Jemmy Lovell? What is the condition of the inhabitants of Boston? Are they suffered to come out? The circumstances of our army, and the intended operations of our forces? are questions I want to have answered. If I am to remain on the *clam banks*, I hope you will take the first opportunity to write me, and give as particular information as possible.

I am, Sir,
Your Friend,
S. PARSONS.

To Capt. Joseph Trumbull,
In Cambridge.

NUMBER VII. Page 30.

The claim that Samuel Adams and John Hancock were at Hartford, and parties to the arrangement by Colonel Parsons and his associates, to send the messengers to the New Hampshire Grants, there to raise men for the expedition against Ticonderoga, rests wholly upon an extract from a letter published in Force's Archives, p. 507, as an "Extract from a letter from a gentleman in Pittsfield to an officer at

Cambridge, May 4, 1775," in which it is said that "the plan was concerted at Hartford last Saturday, by the Governor and Council; Colonel Hancock, and Mr. Adams and others from our Province being present." Mr. J. HAMMOND TRUMBULL, in his concise and excellent paper on the "Origin of the Expedition against Ticonderoga," has clearly shown the error of this statement, and that Mr. Bancroft was misled by it. Saturday was the *twenty-ninth* of April, and on that day, according to Mr. Wells, the biographer of Mr. Adams, the latter, in company with Mr. Hancock, arrived at Hartford, having been at Worcester, on the 27th, as we have already seen. But the expedition originated at Hartford on the 27th. This is shown by the letter from Parsons to Trumbull of June 2, *and the receipts for the money drawn from the treasury of Connecticut are dated on the 28th, before the arrival of Messrs. Hancock and Adams.* Mott says, in his journal, that he arrived at Hartford on the 28th, and that Deane and Parsons wished he "had arrived one day sooner; that they had been on such a plan, and had sent off Messrs. Noah Phelps and Bernard Romans, who they had supplied with £300 cash from the Treasury," etc.; and the journal continues, "Saturday, the 29th April, in the afternoon, we set out on said expedition." It is, therefore, certain that the writer of the Pittsfield letter was in error, and that Adams and Hancock could have had nothing to do with the origin of the expedition, as they did not reach Hartford until two days after the plan was laid, and one day after Phelps and Romans had departed.

This is not the only error which has arisen from these Pittsfield letters, and their incomplete publication by Mr. Force. They were, in fact, written by the *Rev. Thomas Allen*, to General Seth Pomroy, who was then with the army at Cambridge. It is not difficult, now that the authorship of these letters is known, to understand how Mr. Allen fell into his mistake, for such it was, beyond question. Noah Phelps and Romans, who left Hartford with the money, went to Bennington direct. If they passed through Pittsfield, they do not appear to have made any stay there, or to have communicated their mission to any one previous to their arrival on the Grants. Mott and his party left Hartford on Saturday, in the afternoon, and did not reach Pittsfield until the evening of Monday, May 1st. They went direct to Colonel Easton's, with whom they passed the night. Mr. Allen was chairman of the Pittsfield Committee of Safety, and would probably have been consulted by Mott and his party. They left Hartford after Adams and Hancock arrived there, and might naturally have spoken of their arrival in connection with their own expedition. The fact that Phelps and Romans had preceded them by a day, was probably not explained, and thus Mr. Allen was left to infer that the expedition was organized on Saturday, instead of on Thursday. Mott states that he overtook those who had gone forward, after he reached Bennington, except Noah Phelps and a Mr. Hitchcock, who were gone to reconnoiter the fort.

The authorship of the two Pittsfield letters, which are published in a mutilated form in the "Archives," was first determined by *Dr. Field*, in his History of Pittsfield, published in 1844. Both these letters are given in the Appendix to that History. See also No. XIX. of this Appendix.

NUMBER VIII. Page 33.

The journal of Captain Mott contains so clear an account of his part in the expedition against Ticonderoga, that I think it should be given here, notwithstanding its length. I follow the copy in the first volume of the Connecticut Historical Society's Collections.

"PRESTON, Friday, 28th April, 1775.—Set out for Hartford, where I arrived the same day. Saw Christopher Leffingwell, Esq., who enquired of me about the situation of the people of Boston. When I had given him an account, he asked me how they could be relieved, and where I thought we could get artillery and stores. I told him I knew not, except we went and took possession of Ticonderoga and Crown Point, which I thought might be done by surprise, with a small number of men. Mr. Leffingwell left me, and in a short time came to me again, and brought with him Samuel H. Parsons and Silas Deane, Esqs., when he asked me if I would undertake in such an expedition as we had talked of before. I told him I would. They told me they wished I had been there one day sooner; that they had been on such a plan, and that they had sent off Messrs. Noah Phelps and Bernard Romans, who they had supplied with £300, in cash, from the Treasury, and ordered them to draw for more if they should need; that said Phelps and Romans were gone by the way of Salisbury, where they would make a stop; that they expected a small number of men would join them, and if I would go after them, they would give me an order or letter to them, to join with them, and to have my voice with them in conducting the affair and laying out the money; and also, that I might take five or six men with me. On which, I took with me Mr. Jeremiah Halsey, Mr. Epaphras Bull, Mr. Wm. Nichols, Mr. Elijah Babcock, and John Bigelow joined me; and Saturday, the 29th April, in the afternoon, we set out on said expedition. That night arrived at Smith's, in New Hartford; stayed that night. The next day, being Sunday, the 30th April, on our way to Salisbury, Mr. Babcock tired his horse; we got another horse of Esq. Humphrey, in Norfolk, and that day arrived at Salisbury,—tarried all night; and the next day, having augmented our company to the number of sixteen in the whole, we concluded it was not best to add any more, as we meant to keep our business a secret, and ride through the country unarmed till we came to the new settlements on the Grants. We arrived at Mr. Dewey's, in Sheffield, and there we sent off Mr. Jer. Halsey and Capt. John Stephens, to go to Albany, in order to discover the temper of the people in that place, and to return and inform us as soon as possible.

That night we arrived at Col. Easton's, in Pittsfield, where we fell in company with John Brown, Esq., who had been at Canada and Ticonderoga, about a month before, on which we concluded to make known our business to Col. Easton and said Brown, and to take their advice on the same. I was advised by Messrs. Deane, Leffingwell and Parsons, at Hartford, not to raise our men till we came to the N. Hampshire Grants, lest we should be discovered by having too long a march through the country; but when we advised with said Easton and Brown, they advised us that, as there was a great scarcity of provisions in the Grants, and as the people were generally poor, it would be difficult to get a sufficient number of men there; therefore, we had better raise a number of men sooner. Said Easton and Brown concluded to go with us, and Easton said he would assist me in raising some men in his regiment. We then concluded for me to go with Col. Easton to Jericho and Williamstown, to raise men, and the rest of us to go forward to Bennington, and see if they could purchase provisions there. We raised 24 men in Jericho, and 15 in Williamstown, and got them equipped, ready to march. Then Col. Easton and I set out for Bennington. That evening, we met with an express from our people, informing us that they had seen a man directly from Ticonderoga, and that he informed them that they were reinforced at Ticonderoga, and were repairing the garrison, and were every way on their guard; therefore, it was best for us to dismiss the men we had raised, and proceed no further, as we should not succeed. I asked who the man was, where he belonged, and where he was going, but could get no account; on which I ordered that the men should not be dismissed, but that we would proceed.

The next day I arrived at Bennington; there, overtook our people,—all but Noah Phelps and Mr. Heacock, who were gone forward to reconnoiter the fort, and Mr. Halsey and Mr. Stephens had not got back from Albany. I inquired why they sent back to me to dismiss the expedition, when neither our men from Albany, nor the reconnoitering party had returned? They said that they did not think that we should succeed. I told them that fellow they saw knew nothing about the garrison; that I had seen him since, and had examined him strictly, and that he was a lying fellow, and had not been at the fort. I told them, with the two hundred men that we proposed to raise, I was not afraid to go round the fort in open light; if it was reinforced with five hundred men, they would not follow us out into the woods; that the accounts we had would not do to go back with, and tell in Hartford. While on this discourse, Mr. Halsey and Stephens came back from Albany, and both agreed with me, that it was best to go forward; after which, Mr. Halsey and Mr. Bull both declared that they would go back for no story, 'till they had seen the fort for themselves. On which it was concluded that we would proceed; and, as provisions were very scarce on the Grants, we sent Capt. Stephens and Mr. Hewitt to Albany, New City, to purchase provisions, and send to us as soon as they could; and Mr. Romans left us, and joined no more. We were all glad, as he had been a trouble to us all the time he was with us.

Then we proceeded to raise men as fast as possible, and sent forward men on whom we could depend, to waylay the roads that lead from those places we were raising men in, to Fort Edward, Lake George, Skenesborough, Ticonderoga or Crown Point, with orders to take up all those who were passing from either of these garrisons, and send to us to be examined; and that all who were passing towards these garrisons, from us, should be stopped, so that no intelligence should go from us to the garrisons; and, on Sunday night, the seventh of May, we all arrived at Cassel Town (Castleton), the place where we had appointed for the men all to meet; and on Monday, the 8th of May, the Committee all got together, to conclude in what method we would proceed, in order to accomplish our design, of which Committee I was chairman.

And, after debating on the different methods to proceed, and in what manner to retreat, in case of a repulse, we resolved and voted, that we would proceed in the following manner, viz.: That a party of thirty men, under the command of

Capt. Herrick, should, the next day, in the afternoon, take into custody Major Skene and his party, and boats; and that the rest of the men, which consisted of about 140, should go through Shoreham to the lake, opposite to Ticonderoga; and that a part of the men that went to Skenesborough should, in the night following, go down the lake, by Ticonderoga, in the boats, to Shoreham, in order to carry men across the lake to Ticonderoga. We also sent Capt. Douglass to go to Crown Point, and see if he could not agree with his brother-in-law, who lived there, to hire the king's boats, on some stratagem, and send up the lake from there, to assist in carrying over our men. It was further agreed that Col. Ethan Allen should have the command of the party that should go against Ticonderoga, agreeable to my promise made to the men when I engaged them to go, that they should be commanded by their own officers.

In the evening, after the party that was to go to Skenesborough was drafted out, and Col. Allen was gone to Mr. Wessell's, in Shoreham, to meet some men who were to come in there, having received his orders, at what time he must be ready, and must take possession of the garrison of Ticonderoga,—the whole plan being settled by a vote of the Committee.

In the evening, Col. Arnold came to us, with his orders, and demanded the command of our people, as he said we had no proper orders. We told him we could not surrender the command to him, as our people were raised on condition that they should be commanded by their own officers. He persisted in his demand, and the next morning he proceeded forward to overtake Col. Allen. I was then with the party that was going to Skenesborough, a mile and a half distance from the other party. When Col. Arnold went after Col. Allen, the whole party followed him, for fear he should prevail on Col. Allen to resign the command, and left all the provisions, so that I, with Capt. Phelps and Babcock, was obliged to leave the party that I was with, and go with the pack-horses with the provisions, and could not overtake them till the first division had crossed the lake. We followed them, as soon as the boats got back, and when we got over, they were in possession of the fort. We entered the fort immediately, and soon got the Regular troops under guard, and their arms all in our possession. This was done on Wednesday, the 10th of May. After which, Col. Arnold challenged the command again, and insisted that he had a right to have it; on which, our soldiers again paraded, and declared that they would go right home, for they would not be commanded by Arnold. We told them they should not, and at length pacified them; and then reasoned with Arnold, and told him, *as he had not raised any men, he could not expect to have the command of ours.* He still insisted that, as we had no legal orders to show, he had a right to take the command. On which I wrote Col. Allen his orders, as followeth, viz.:

To Col. Ethan Allen:—

SIR,—*Whereas*, agreeable to the Power and Authority to us given by the COLONY OF CONNECTICUT, we have appointed you to take the command of a party of men, and reduce and take possession of the garrison of Ticonderoga and its dependencies. And, as you are now in possession of the same, you are hereby

8

directed to keep the command of said garrison, for the use of the American Colonies, till you have further orders from the Colony of Connecticut, or from the Continental Congress.

Signed per order of the Committee,
EDWARD MOTT, *Chairman of Committee.*"

Ticonderoga, May 10th, 1775.

NUMBER IX. *Page* 83.

The Rev. *Thomas Allen* was one of the most active patriots in Western Massachusetts. He was a native of Northampton, and the first minister settled in Pittsfield. On the 30th of June, 1774, he was made Chairman of a Standing Committee of Safety and Correspondence for the town, in which position his correspondence exhibits great vigilance and zeal in the Revolutionary cause. He was active in promoting the expedition against Ticonderoga, and the next year he acted as chaplain in the army, at White Plains, under Washington, and afterwards officiated in the same capacity at Ticonderoga. In August, 1777, he went with a volunteer company of militia from Pittsfield to Bennington, and took an active part in the battle that ensued. "Reporting himself to General Stark, he was forthwith appointed chaplain, and there are those who yet express their belief in the efficacy of a prayer before the army, on the morning of the action, which ascended from the fervent lips of Mr. Allen. Among the reinforcements from Berkshire County, says Edward Everett, in his Life of Stark, came a clergyman, with a portion of his flock, resolved to make bare the arm of flesh against the enemies of his country. Before daylight, on the morning of the 16th, he addressed the Commander as follows: 'We, the people of Berkshire, have frequently been called upon to fight, but have never been led against the enemy. We have now resolved, if you will not let us fight, never to turn out again.' General Stark asked him 'If he wished to march then, when it was dark and raining?' 'No,' was the answer. 'Then,' continued Stark, 'if the Lord should once more give us sunshine, and I do not give you fighting enough, I will never ask you to come again!' The weather cleared up in the course of the day, and the men of Berkshire followed their spiritual guide into action.

Before the attack was commenced, being posted opposite to that wing of the enemy which was principally composed of refugees, who had joined the invaders, Mr. Allen advanced in front of our militia, and in a voice distinctly heard by them, exhorted the enemy to lay down their arms, assuring them of good quarters, and warning them of the consequences of refusal. Having performed what he considered a religious duty, and being fired upon, he resumed his place in the ranks, and, when the signal was given, was among the foremost in attacking the enemy.

There is a tradition that Mr. Allen was recognized by some of these refugees; for there were a very few men of this description from Pittsfield and other parts of Berkshire, and that they said: "There is Parson Allen; let us pop him!" There is also a tradition, that when he was fired upon, and the bullets of the enemy where whistling about him, he jumped down from the rock or stump on which he had stood, and cried out: "Now, boys, let us give it to them!" and immediately said to his brother Joseph, by his side: "You load, and I will fire!" Being asked whether he killed a man, he replied: "He did not know; but that observing a flash often repeated in a bush near by, which seemed to be succeeded each time by a fall of some of our men, he levelled his musket, and firing in that direction, *he put out that flash!*"

Dr. Field, from whose sketch of Pittsfield the foregoing is extracted, says that Mr. Allen continued in the ministry until his death, which took place on the 11th of February, 1810, at the age of sixty-seven years.

He had twelve children, nine sons and three daughters. One of his sons, Rev. William Allen, D. D., succeeded his father in the ministry at Pittsfield, and was the author of Allen's Biographical Dictionary. Another son, Solomon Metcalf Allen, a graduate of Middlebury in 1813, studied Theology, but was appointed Professor of the Ancient Languages, at Middlebury, in 1816, and lost his life by an accident in the following year.

NUMBER X. *Page* 37.

Major Gershom Beach, of Rutland, Vermont, was one of the most earnest and energetic of the Green Mountain Boys. After the arrival of the expedition at Shoreham, Captain Noah Phelps, of Simsbury, Conn., who had been sent forward to reconnoitre the fort, joined the party, and reported that the fort was in a comparatively defenseless condition,—the men not being on their guard, and their ammunition damaged. Allen immediately dispatched Major Beach to collect men, and direct them to join the expedition at Hand's Point. Goodhue, in his "History of Shoreham," p. 13, says: "Beach went on foot to Rutland, Pittsford, Brandon, Middlebury, Whiting and Shoreham, making a circuit of sixty miles in twenty-four hours."

Major Beach was an intimate friend of Major Skene, and was at Skenesborough on Saturday before Skene was captured. The Major consulted with Beach about rebuilding the forts at Ticonderoga, Crown Point, etc., and told him his father was coming out with a commission as Governor of the country, and authority to repair all the defenses. Beach replied that he thought he would have difficulty in raising men, as the men would *have business at Boston!* Skene was soon relieved of all difficulty on this score, for on the following Tuesday he was captured and sent to Connecticut.

NUMBER XI. *Page* 42.

The following extract is taken from Zadock Thompson's "Gazetteer of Vermont," Part Second, p. 33:

"While they were collecting at Castleton, Colonel Arnold arrived there, attended only by a servant. This officer had been chosen captain by an independant company at New Haven, in Connecticut, and, as soon as he heard of the battle at Lexington, he marched his company to Cambridge, where the Americans were assembling to invest Boston. There, he received a colonel's commission from the Massachusetts Committee of Safety, with orders to raise four hundred men for the reduction of Ticonderoga and Crown Point, which he represented to be in a ruinous condition, and feebly garrisoned. His commission being examined, Arnold was permitted to join the party; but it was ordered by a council that Allen should also have the commission of Colonel, and should be first in command.

"To procure intelligence, Captain Noah Phelps, one of the gentlemen from Connecticut, went into the fort at Ticonderoga, in the habit of one of the settlers, where he enquired for a barber, under the pretence of wanting to be shaved. By affecting an awkward appearance, and asking many simple questions, he passed unsuspected, and had a favorable opportunity of observing the condition of the works. Having obtained the necessary information, he returned to the party, and the same night they began their march for the fort. And these affairs had been conducted with so much expedition, that Allen reached Orwell, opposite to Ticonderoga, with his men, in the evening of the 9th of May, while the garrison were without any knowledge of the proceedings, and without any apprehension of a hostile visit.

"The whole force collected on this occasion amounted to 270 men, of whom 230 were Green Mountain Boys. It was with difficulty that boats could be obtained to carry over the troops. A Mr. Douglass was sent to Bridport to procure aid in men, and a scow belonging to Mr. Smith. Douglass stopped by the way to enlist a Mr. Chapman in the enterprise, when James Wilcox and Joseph Tyler, two young men who were a-bed in the chamber, hearing the story, conceived the design of decoying on shore a large oar-boat belonging to Major Skene, and which then lay off against Willow Point. They dressed, seized their guns and jug of rum, of which they knew the black commander to be extremely fond,—gathered four men as they went, and arriving all armed, they hailed the boat, and offered to help row it to Shoreham, if he would carry them immediately, to join a hunting party that would be waiting for them. The stratagem succeeded, and poor Jack and his two men suspected nothing, till they arrived at Allen's headquarters, and were made prisoners of war.

Douglass arrived with the scow about the same time, and some other boats having been collected, Allen embarked with 83 men, and landed near the fort."

The *Willow Point*, near which Major Skene's boat lay, must not be confounded with another point of the same name, about a half mile north of the fort, upon which Allen and his men made their landing. The first Willow Point is on the eastern, or Vermont shore, nearly opposite Crown Point, and in the northwesterly corner of the town of Bridport. The other is on the west, or New York side, a little south of Hand's Cove, where the expedition embarked.—*See Goodhue's Hist. Shoreham, p. 16.*

NUMBER XII, Page 44.

There has been much confusion in relation to the true date of the capture of Crown Point. Arnold, writing to the Massachusetts Committee of Safety, on the 11th, says:

"The party I advised were gone to Crown Point, are returned, having met with head winds, and that expedition, and taking the sloop, is *entirely laid aside.*" Arnold must have known this statement to be false when he penned it. Ira Allen, who was in the expedition against Ticonderoga, in his "History of Vermont," p. 59, says, after describing the capture of Ticonderoga, "a party was sent by water, as soon as possible, to Crown Point, under the command of Captain Warner. Previous to this, Colonel Allen had sent orders to Captain Baker, of Onion River, forty miles north of Crown Point, to come with his company and assist; and, though belated, yet he met and took two small boats on their way to give the alarm to Fort St. John. Captain Warner and Baker appeared before Crown Point nearly at the same time; the garrison, having only few men, surrendered without opposition." It has been commonly supposed that Warner left on the morning of the 10th, soon after the capture of Ticonderoga, and that Crown Point was taken on the same day. The following letter, however, now in the possession of Hon. L. Hebard, of Lebanon, Conn., just published in "The Dartmouth Magazine," for May, 1872, fixes the date of the capture of Crown Point beyond question:

"HEAD QUARTERS, CROWN POINT, 12th May, 1775.

GENT.—*Yesterday*, we took possession of this garrison in the name of the country,—we found great quantyties of ordnance, stores, &c. Very little provision. We have had parties out several days, watching every passage to Canady, by land and water. Have taken two mails; have not examined them very particularly; find nothing material in English,—some letters in French and High Dutch which we could not read. The bearer, Mr. Levi Allen, has this moment returned from a party that was watching the lake, to stop any news going to Canady, as we want to have sloop return from St. Johns, and make a *prize* of her. She will be well loaded. Allen informs us a bark canoe has been seen standing for Canady, three miles north of his station on the lake, by which means, we suppose, Gov. Carlton will hear what we have done, before this comes to hand. He is a man-of-war; you can guess what measures he will take. We determine to fight them three to one, but he can bring ten to one, and more. We should be glad of assistance of men, provisions and powder, and beg your advice whether we shall abandon this place and retire to Ticonderoga, or proceed to St. Johns, &c., &c. The latter we should be fondest of. We are, Gen'l., yours to command,

SETH WARNER,
PELEG SUNDERLAND,

To His Hon. the Governor and Council
and Gen. Assembly Connecticut."

NUMBER XIII. Page 44.

ETHAN ALLEN TO THE ALBANY COMMITTEE.

TICONDEROGA, May 11th, 1775.

GENTLEMEN:—I have the inexpressible satisfaction to acquaint you, that, at daybreak of the tenth instant, pursuant to my directions from sundry leading gentlemen of *Massachusetts Bay* and *Connecticut*, I took the fortress of *Ticonderoga*, with about one hundred and thirty *Green Mountain Boys*. Colonel *Easton*, with about forty-seven valiant soldiers, distinguished themselves in the action. Colonel *Arnold* entered the fortress with me, side by side. The guard was so surprised, that contrary to expectation, they did not fire on us, but retreated with precipitancy. We immediately entered the fortress, and took the garrison prisoners, without bloodshed or any opposition. They consisted of one captain and a lieutenant, and forty-two men.

Little more need be said. You know Governour *Carlton*, of *Canada*, will exert himself to retake it; and, as your county is nearer than any other part of the Colonies, and as your inhabitants have thoroughly manifested their zeal in the cause of the country, I expect immediate assistance from you, both in men and provisions. You cannot exert yourself too much in so glorious a cause. The number of men need be more at first, till the other Colonies can have time to muster. I am apprehensive of a sudden and quick attack. Pray be quick to our relief, and send us five hundred men immediately; fail not.

From your friend and humble servant,

ETHAN ALLEN, *Commander of Ticonderoga.*

ABRAHAM YATES, Chairman of the Committee, *Albany.*

NUMBER XIV. *Page* 48.

ETHAN ALLEN TO THE MASSACHUSETTS CONGRESS.

TICONDEROGA, May 11, 1775.

GENTLEMEN:—

I have to inform you, with pleasure unfelt before, that on the break of day of tenth of *May*, 1775, by the order of the General Assembly of the Colony of *Connecticut*, I took the Fortress of *Ticonderoga* by storm. The soldiery was composed of about one hundred *Green Mountain Boys*, and near fifty veteran soldiers from the Province of *Massachusetts Bay*. The latter was under the command of Colonel *James Easton*, who behaved with great zeal and fortitude,—not only in council, but in the assault. The soldiery behaved with such resistless fury, that they so terrified the King's troops, that they durst not fire on their assailants, and our soldiery was agreeably disappointed. The soldiery behaved with uncommon rancour when they leaped into the Fort; and, it must be confessed, that the Colonel has greatly contributed to the taking of that fortress, as well as *John Brown*, Esq., attorney at law, who was also an able counsellor, and was personally in the attack. I expect the Colonies will maintain this fort. As to the cannon and warlike stores, I hope they may serve the cause of liberty, instead of tyranny, and I humbly implore your assistance in immediately assisting the Government of *Connecticut* in establishing a garrison in the reduced premises. Colonel *Easton* will inform you at large. From, gentlemen, your most obedient, humble servant,

ETHAN ALLEN.

To the Honorable Congress of the Province } of *Massachusetts Bay*, or Council of War. }

NUMBER XV. Page 50.

COLONEL ETHAN ALLEN TO GOVERNOR TRUMBULL.

TICONDEROGA, 12th May, 1775.

HON'BLE SIR :—I make you a present of a Major, a Captain and two Lieutenants in the regular Establishment of George the Third. I hope they may serve as ransoms for some of our friends at Boston, and particularly for Capt. Brown, of Rhode Island. A party of men, under the command of Capt. Herrick, has took possession of Skenesborough, imprisoned Major Skene, and seized a schooner of his. I expect, in ten days' time, to have it rigged, manned and armed with six or eight pieces of cannon, which, with the boats in our possession, I purpose to make an attack on the armed sloop of George the Third, which is now cruising on Lake Champlain, and is about twice as big as the schooner. I hope in a short time to be authorized to acquaint your Honour, that Lake Champlain, and the fortifications thereon, are subject to the Colonies.

The enterprise has been approbated by the officers and soldiery of the Green Mountain Boys, nor do I hesitate as to the success. I expect lives must be lost in the attack, as the commander of George's sloop is a man of courage, etc.

Messrs. Hickok, Halsey and Nichols have the charge of conducting the officers to Hartford. These gentlemen have been very assiduous and active in the late expedition.

I depend upon your Honour's aid and assistance in a situation so contiguous to Canada.

I subscribe myself, your Honour's ever faithful,
Most obedient and humble Servant,
ETHAN ALLEN, *At present Commander of Ticonderoga.*

To the Hon'ble JONATHAN TRUMBULL, Esq.,
Capt. General and Governour of the Colony of Connecticut.

COMMISSARY ELISHA PHELPS TO GENERAL ASSEMBLY OF CONNECTICUT.

SKENESBOROUGH, May 16th, 1775.

To the Honorable General Assembly of the Colony of Connecticut, in New England, America, now sitting at Hartford:

GENTLEMEN OF THE HOUSE :—I now would endeavor to state before you the situation of affairs of these northern frontiers, and the army and fort, and our proceedings from the beginning. When we left Hartford, our orders was to repair to the Grants of New Hampshire, and raise an army of men, as we thought proper, to go and take the Fort Ticonderoga and Crown Point, and Major Skene, etc., and to destroy the fort, or keep it, and send an express to Albany, and see if they would keep it; or send to the Colony of Connecticut. Upon which orders we went to Pittsfield, and Col. Easton and Capt. Douglass [Dickenson?] joined us with about sixty men; and we pursued to Bennington, and met Col. Allen, who was much pleased with the intended expedition, and we agreed he should get one hundred men. We sent forward to Crown Point and Ticondcroga, Capt. Noah Phelps and Mr. Hickok, to reconnoitre and see what discovery they could make who met us at Castleton—who informed us that the regulars was not any ways apprised of our coming. To which, the army pursued on, and on the 10th day of May Instant, took Fort Ticonderoga, and also Major Skene, and have sent them, with proper guards, to Hartford. There is, at the fort, about 200 men,—in a fort of broken walls and gates, and but few cannon in order, and very much out of repair,—and in a great quarrel with Col. Arnold, who shall command the fort, even that some of the soldiers threaten the life of Col. Arnold. Major Skene's estate we have put into the care of Capt. Noah Lee, a man of good character, and capable of taking care of the business well. The people on the Grants are in much distress for want of provisions. The iron work must be carried on for the benefit of the people here; but it would not do, by no means, to have Mr. Brook stay here, as he was looked upon to be a bigger enemy to his country than Major Skene, and 'tis an easy matter to send an Indian to Canada, and inform them all our schemes and plans. One enemy in the city is worse than ten outside.

Nows I have, by a credible man as any in these parts (by name, Gershom Beach, of Rutland), and who has been one of Major Skene's best friends, but loves himself and country better,—who told me he was at the Major's on Saturday, before the Major was taken (who was taken Tuesday); that his father had sent him a letter, and shewed it to him, which informed the young Major that he had married to a lady of fortune, of forty-three thousand pound sterling, and that he had a commission in chief over Fort Ticonderoga and Crown Point and Fort George; also, the Major asked Mr. Beach about rebuilding the forts. Mr. Beach told him he could not get men enough, as they would be at Boston. The Major replied, his father had a thousand men coming with him, and was to have been here by the first day of May instant. Now, gentlemen, I must beg liberty to offer my humble opinion, which is, that not less than three thousand men be sent here immediately, and to push on to St. Johns and Canada, and secure them forts, and, in doing that, secure the Canadians and Indians on our side, and rescue the frontier from the rage of the savages; and for another small army to go to Detroit, etc. Begging pardon for directing any in these affairs.

Now, gentlemen, as we have done the business we was sent to do, must pray that you would send me special orders, whether I should provide any longer for the army, on the Colony of Connecticut's cost, or not. As I was appointed by the Committee, of which I had the honor to be one, to be commissary of the army, I am determined to go to New City and Albany, and secure some provision, and wait for further orders from the Assembly.

I dined with three Indians this day, who belonged to Stockbridge, sent by Mr. Edwards, and a number of other gentlemen of that town, to Canada, to see if they can find out the temper of the Canada Indians. I also saw a young gentleman from Albany, that says they disapproved of our proceeding in taking the fort, in that we did not acquaint them of it before that it was done. Perhaps it would be well if some gentlemen should wait on the Congress at New York, so as to keep peace with them. N. B. We did inform the Gentlemen Committee of Albany of our proceedings, which you will see by a letter in the hands of Capt. Mott.

Gentlemen, I am, with esteem, your very humble Servant to command,

ELISHA PHELPS."

It would, probably, have saved the Colonies the disasters of the next autumn and winter, including the loss of General Montgomery and the greater part of his army, if the earnest counsels of this letter, and of Ethan Allen, in favor of an immediate invasion of Canada, had been followed. There seems little doubt that the people of Canada sympathized with the movements of the Colonies, and might easily have been induced to join with them in resistance to Great Britain. But the Continental Congress was not ripe for such a movement. It even apologized to the people of Canada for the capture of Ticonderoga, and, on the 29th of May, adopted an address to them, in which they say, "that the taking of the fort and military stores at Ticonderoga and Crown Point, and the armed vessels on the lake, was dictated by the great law of self-preservation. They were intended to annoy us, and to cut off that friendly intercourse and communication which has hitherto subsisted between us. We hope it has given you no uneasiness," etc. And, on the first of June, the same Congress resolved, "That no expedition or incursion ought to be undertaken or made by any Colony, or body of Colonists, against or into Canada." An invasion at that time would probably have met with little active resistance.

The elder Skene, referred to in the foregoing letter, was captured on the arrival of the vessel from London in which he took passage, and sent to Philadelphia. On the 8th of June, the Continental Congress being informed "that the said Skene has lately been appointed Governor of the Forts of Ticonderoga and Crown Point," and apprehending that he was "a dangerous partisan of Administration," appointed a committee to examine his papers; and, on the 5th of July, "it appearing that Gov. Philip Skene and Mr. Lundy have designs inimical to America," they were ordered to be sent to Connecticut, and placed in charge of Gov. Trumbull, as prisoners of war.—*See Journals of Cont. Congress*, 1775, pp. 114, 142.

NUMBER XVI. Page 51.

See American Bibliopolist, Vol. III., No. 36, p. 491. Dec. 1871.

This account, published in the *Worcester Spy*, May 17, 1755, endorsed by the editor as being "furnished by a correspondent whose veracity can be depended upon," is probably the *earliest published cotemporary account of the capture*. It is one week earlier than that of Colonel Easton in the same newspaper, and appears to be the source from which the London magazines of the time made up their items. The *Bibliopolist* is entitled to the credit of reproducing a piece of important evidence, which has not been cited since the controversy respecting Ticonderoga has arisen. The account is as follows:

"Col. James Easton and Col. Ethan Allen, having raised about 150 men for the purpose, agreeable to a plan formed in Connecticut, detached a party of about thirty men to go to Skenesborough, and take into custody Major Skene and his party of regular soldiers; and, with the remainder, having crossed the lake in boats in the night, and landed about half a mile from said fortress, immediately marched, with great silence, to the gates of the fortress, and at break of day, May 10th, made the assault with great intrepidity,—our men darting like lightning upon the guards, gave them but just time to snap two guns at our men before they took them prisoners. This was immediately followed by the reduction of the fort and its dependencies. About 40 of the King's troops are taken prisoners (including one captain, one lieutenant, and inferior officers), with a number of women and children belonging to the soldiery at this garrison. Major Skene and the whole of his party are also taken. The prisoners are now under guard, on their way to Hartford, where it is probable they will arrive the latter end of this week. Those who took an account of the ordinance, warlike stores, etc., judged it amounted to no less than £300,000 in value. A party was immediately detached to take possession of Crown Point, where no great opposition was expected to be made. As the possession of this place affords us a key to all Canada, and may be of infinite importance to us in future, it must rejoice the hearts of all lovers of their country, that so noble an acquisition was made without the loss of one life, and is certainly an encomium upon the wisdom and valour of the New Englanders, however some tories would fain insinuate that they will not fight nor encounter danger.

☞ *What think ye of the Yankees now?*

We are told there are about 100 pieces of cannon, from 6 to 24 pounders at Ticonderoga."

NUMBER XVII. *Page* 52.

PETITION OF CAPTAIN DELAPLACE.

To the Honorable, the General Assembly of the Governour and Company of the ENGLISH *Colony of* CONNECTICUT, *in* NEW ENGLAND, *in* AMERICA, *now convened at* HARTFORD:

The memorial of *William Delaplace*, a Captain in His Majesty's Twenty-Sixth Regiment, and Commandant of the Fort and garrison of *Ticonderoga*, in behalf of himself and the officers and soldiers under his command, beg leave to represent our difficult situation to your Honours, and petition for redress.

Your memorialist would represent, that on the morning of the tenth of *May* instant, the garrison of the Fortress of Tionderoga, in the Province of New York, was surprised by a party of armed men, under the command of one *Ethan Allen*, consisting of about one hundred and fifty, who had taken such measures effectually to surprise the same, that very little resistance could be made, and to whom your memorialists were obliged to surrender as prisoners; and overpowered by a superior force, and disarmed, and by said *Allen* ordered immediately to be sent to Hartford, in the Colony of Connecticut, where your memorialists are detained as prisoners of war,—consisting of officers, forty-seven private soldiers of His Majesty's troops, besides women and children. That your memorialists, being ignorant of any crime by them committed, whereby they should be thus taken and held, also are ignorant by what authority said *Allen* thus took them, or that they are thus detained in a strange country, and at a distance from the post assigned them; thus know not in what light they are considered by your Honours consequently know not what part to act; would therefore ask your Honours' interposition and protection, and order that they be set at liberty, to return to the post from whence they were taken, or to join the regiment to which thy belong; or, if they are considered in the light of prisoners of war, your Honours would be pleased to signify the same to them, and by whom they are detained, and that your Honours would afford us your favor and protection during the time we shall tarry in this Colony; and your memorialists shall ever pray.

        WILLIAM DELAPLACE,
         Captain, Commandant Ticonderoga Fort.

HARTFORD, May 24, 1775.

NUMBER XVIII. *Page* 52.

"AUTHENTICK ACCOUNT OF THE TAKING OF FORTRESSES AT TICONDEROGA AND CROWN POINT BY A PARTY OF THE CONNECTICUT FORCES.

         "NEW YORK, May 18, 1775.

"Captain *Edward Mott* and Captain *Noah Phelps* set out from *Hartford* on *Saturday*, the twenty-ninth of *April*, in order to take possession of the Fortress of *Ticonderoga*, and the dependencies thereto belonging. They took with them from *Connecticut* sixteen men unarmed, and marched privately through the country till they came to *Pittsfield*, without discovering their design to any person, till they fell in company with Colonel *Ethan Allen*, Colonel *Easton*, and *John Brown*, Esq., who engaged to join themselves to said *Mott* and *Phelps*, and to raise men sufficient to take the place by surprise, if possible. Accordingly, the men were raised, and proceeded, as directed by said *Mott* and *Phelps*, Colonel *Ethan Allen* commanding the soldiery. On *Tuesday*, they surprised and took the fortress, making prisoners the Commandant and his party. On *Wednesday* morning they possessed themselves of *Crown Point*, taking possession of the ordinance stores, consisting of upwards of two hundred pieces of cannon, three mortars, sundry howitzers, and fifty swivels, etc.

"*Ethan Allen*, fearful of an attempt from Governour *Carleton* to retake the place, has written to the Committee of *Albany* for a supply of five hundred men and provisions. The Committee, however, not perceiving themselves competent to determine on a matter of so much importance, requested the advice of our General Committee, who referred them, and immediately despatched an express, to the Congress now sitting at *Philadelphia.*"

NUMBERS XIX. and XX. *Page* 54.

See Number VII. of this Appendix, where the authorship of this letter is referred to. The letter of May 9th, written by Rev. Thomas Allen to General Pomeroy, is given in such an imperfect form in the "Archives," that I give it here in full from Dr. Field's "History of Pittsfield," p. 75. The portions italicised are omitted by Mr. Force, who probably follows a copy published at the time. The importance of the concluding paragraph is apparent.

"PITTSFIELD, May 9th, 1775.

GEN. POMEROY—SIR:

I shall esteem it a great happiness if I can communicate any intelligence to you, Sir, that shall be of any service to my country. In my last, I wrote to you of the northern expedition. Before the week ends, we are in raised hopes, here, of hearing that Ticonderoga and Crown Point are in other hands. *Whether the expedition fails or succeeds, I will send you the most early intelligence, as I look on it as an affair of great importance.* Solomon, the Indian king, at Stockbridge, was lately at Col. Easton's, of this town, and said there that the Mohawks had not only gave liberty to the Stockbridge Indians to join us, but had sent them a belt, denoting that they would hold in readiness 500 men, to join us immediately on the first notice, and that the said Solomon holds an Indian post in actual readiness to run with the news as soon as they shall be wanted. *Should the Council of War judge it necessary to send to them, after being better informed of the matter, by Captain Goodrich, now in the service, if you should issue out your orders to. Col. Easton, I make no doubt that he could bring them down soon.* These Indians might be of great service, should the King's troops march out of Boston, as some think they undoubtedly will, upon the arrival of the recruits, and give no (us ?) battle.

Our militia, this way, Sir, are vigorously preparing for actual readiness. Adjacent towns, and this town, are buying arms and ammunition. There is a plenty of arms to be sold at Albany, as yet, but we hear, by order of the Mayor, etc., no powder is to be sold, for the present, there. The spirit of liberty runs high there, as you have doubtless heard by their post to our head quarters. I have exerted myself to disseminate the same spirit in King's District, which has of late taken a surprising effect. The poor Tories at Kinderhook are mortified and grieved, and are wheeling about, and begin to take the quick step. New York Government begins to be alive in the glorious cause, and to act with great vigor. *Some, this way, say that the King's troops will carry off all the plate, merchandize and plunder of the town of Boston, to pay them for their ignominious expedition, which, in my opinion, would not be at all inconsistent with the shameful principles of those who have sent them on so inglorious an expedition.*

I fervently pray, Sir, that our Council of War may be inspired with wisdom from above, to direct the warlike enterprise with prudence, discretion and vigor. O! may your councils and deliberations be under the guidance and blessing of Heaven! Since I began, an intelligible person, who left Ticonderoga Saturday before last, informs me, that having went through there and Crown Point about three weeks ago, all were secure; but, on his return, he found they were alarmed with our expedition, and would not admit him into the fort; that there were twelve soldiers at Crown Point, and he judged near two hundred at Ticonderoga; that these forts are out of repair, and much in ruins; that it was his own opinion our men would undoubtedly be able to take them; and that he met our men last Thursday, who were well furnished with cattle, and wagons laden with provisions, and in good spirits, who, he supposed, would arrive there last Sabbath day, and he doubted not but this week they would be in possession of those forts. He informed them where they might obtain a plenty of ball, and there are cannon enough at Crown Point, which they cannot secure from us; that he saw the Old Sow from Cape Breton, and a number of good brass cannon, at Ticonderoga. Should this expedition succeed, and should the Council of War send up their orders for the people this way to transport by land twenty or thirty of the best cannon to headquarters, I doubt not but the people in this country would do it with all expedition. We could easily collect a thousand yoke of cattle for the business.

Since I wrote the last paragraph, an express has arrived from Benedict Arnold, Commander of the forces against Ticonderoga, for recruits; in consequence of which, orders are issued out for a detachment of eighteen men of each company in this regiment to march immediately, who will be on their way this day. I am, Sir, with great respect, your obedient Servant,

THOMAS ALLEN."

I am aware that it has been generally assumed that Arnold went through the towns in Western Massachusetts, and arranged with officers there to enlist his men. Sparks, in his Life of Allen (Am. Biog., Vol. I., p. 278), says that "Arnold had agreed with officers in Stockbridge to enlist and forward such (men) as could be obtained, making all haste himself to join the expedition, which he did not hear was on foot until he came to that town." *Smith*, in his "History of Pittsfield," Vol. I., p. 219, says that Arnold "is said to have authorized enlistments in Stockbridge; but, on reaching Pittsfield, he learned of the expedition which was anticipating him, and hastened to overtake it." But I am not aware of any evidence proving that he passed through either of these towns. I therefore place Arnold's letter from Rupert in contrast with Mr. Allen's from Pittsfield, and leave the reader to judge for himself whether the inference of the Text is well founded. For myself, I do not believe that he could have passed through Pittsfield, and commenced enlistments there without the knowledge of Mr. Allen, the Chairman of the Pittsfield Committee. If he had done so, *I do not believe he would have sent back an express from Rupert, to the towns in which he had commenced his enlistments, with the following letter,* first published by Mr. Smith, in his "History of Pittsfield:"

RUPORT, 8th May, 1775.

Gentlemen :—By the last information I can get, there is one hundred men, or more, at Ticonderoga, who are alarmed and keep a good look out. I am also informed the sloop has gone to St. Johns for provisions; that she had six guns mounted, and twenty men. We have only one hundred and fifty men gone on, which are not sufficient to secure the vessels and keep the lakes; this ought, by all means, to be done, that we may cut off their communication, and stop all supplies going to the fort, until we can have a sufficient number of men from the lower towns.

I beg the favor of you, gentlemen, as far down as this reaches, to exert yourselves, and send forward as many men to join the army here as you can possibly spare. There is plenty of provisions engaged, and on the road, for five hundred men six or eight weeks. Let every man bring as much powder and ball as he can; also a blanket. Their wages are 40s. per month, I humbly engaged to see paid; also the blankets.

I am, Gentlemen, your humble Servant,
BENEDICT ARNOLD,
Commander of the Forces.

To the Gentlemen in the Southern Towns.

NUMBER XXI. *Page* 56.

BENEDICT ARNOLD TO THE COMMITTEE OF SAFETY.

TICONDEROGA, May 11, 1775.

Gentlemen :—I wrote you yesterday, that, arriving in the vicinity of this place, I found one hundred and fifty men, collected at the instance of some gentlemen from *Connecticut* (designed on the same errand on which I came), headed by Colonel *Ethan Allen*, and that I had joined them, not thinking proper to await the arrival of the troops I had engaged on the road, but to attempt the fort by surprise; that we had taken the fort at four o'clock yesterday morning, without opposition, and had made prisoners, one Captain, one Lieutenant, and forty odd privates and subalterns, and that we found the fort in a most ruinous condition, and not worth repairing. That a party of fifty men were gone to *Crown Point*, and that I intended to follow with as many men, to seize the sloop, etc.; and that I intended to keep possession here until I had further advice from you. On and before our taking possession here, I had agreed with Colonel *Allen* to issue for the orders jointly, until I could raise a sufficient number of men to relieve his people, on which plan we proceeded when I wrote you yesterday, since which, Colonel *Allen*, finding he had the ascendency over his people, positively insisted I should have no command, as I had forbid the soldiers plundering and destroying private property. The power is now taken out of my hands, and I am not consulted; nor have I a voice in any matters. There is here, at present, near one hundred men, who are in the greatest confusion and anarchy, destroying and plundering private property, committing every enormity, and paying no attention to publick service. The party I advised were gone to *Crown Point*, are returned, having met with head winds, and that expedition, and taking the sloop (mounted with six guns), is entirely laid aside. There is not the least regularity among the troops, but everything is governed by whim and caprice,—the soldiers threatening to leave the garrison on the least affront. Most of them must return home soon, as their families are suffering. Under our present situation, I believe one hundred men would retake the fortress, and there seems no prospect of things being in a better situation. I have, therefore, thought proper to send an express, advising you of the state of affairs, not doubting you will take the matter into your serious consideration, and order a number of troops to join those I have coming on here; or that you will appoint some other person to take the command of them and this place, as you shall think most proper. Colonel *Allen* is a proper man to head his own wild people, but entirely unacquainted with military service; and as I am the only person who has been legally authorized to take possession of this place, I am determined to insist on my right, and I think it my duty to remain here against all opposition, until I have further orders. I cannot comply with your orders in regard to the cannon, etc., for want of men. I have wrote to the Governor and General Assembly of *Connecticut,* advising them of my appointment, and giving them an exact detail of matters as they stand at present. I should be extremely glad to be honorably acquitted of my commission, and that a proper person might be appointed in my room. But as I have, in consequence of my orders from you, gentlemen, been the first person who entered and took possession of the fort, I shall keep it, at every hazard, until I have further advice and orders from you and the General Assembly of *Connecticut.*

I have the honor to be, Gentlemen, your most obedient, humble Servant,

BENEDICT ARNOLD.

P. S. It is impossible to advise you how many cannon are here and at *Crown Point,* as many of them are buried in the ruins. There is a large number of iron, and some brass, and mortars, etc., lying on the edge of the lake, which, as the lake is high, are covered with water. The confusion we have been in has prevented my getting proper information, further than that there are many cannon shells, mortars, etc., which may be very serviceable to our army at *Cambridge.*

B. A.

NUMBERS XXII and XXIII. *Page* 58.

The proof that the expedition to Crown Point had not "been entirely laid aside," and that Arnold must have known it, is found in No. XII. of this Appendix.

ARNOLD TO MASSACHUSETTS COMMITTEE OF SAFETY.

TICONDEROGA, May 14, 1775.

Gentlemen:—My last was the 11th instant, per express, since which a party of men have seized on *Crown Point,* in which they took eleven prisoners, and found sixty-one pieces of cannon serviceable, and fifty-three unfit for service. I ordered a party to Skenesborough, to take Major *Skene,* who have made him prisoner, and seized a small schooner, which is just arrived here. I intend setting out in her directly, with a battcau and fifty men, to take possession of the sloop, which, we are advised this morning by the post, is at St. Johns, loaded with provisions, etc., waiting a wind for this place. Enclosed is a list of cannon, etc., here, though imperfect, as we have found many pieces not included, and some are on the edge of the lake, covered with water. I am, with the assistance of Mr. *Bernard Romans,* making preparation at *Fort George* for transporting to *Albany* those cannon that will be serviceable to our army at *Cambridge.* I have about one hundred men here, and expect more every minute. Mr. *Allen's* party is decreasing, and the dispute between us subsiding. I am extremely sorry matters have not been transacted with more prudence and judgment. I have done everything in my power, and put up with many insults to preserve peace and serve the publick. I hope soon to be properly released from this troublesome business, that some more proper person may be appointed in my room; till which, I am, very respectfully, gentlemen, your most obedient, humble servant,

BENEDICT ARNOLD.

P. S. Since writing the above, Mr. *Romans* concludes going to Albany to forward carriages for the cannon, etc., and provisions, which will soon be wanted. I beg leave to observe he has been of great service here, and I think him a very spirited, judicious gentleman, who has the service of the country much at heart, and hope he will meet proper encouragement.

B. A.

NUMBER XXIV. Page 62.

MASSACHUSETTS CONGRESS TO BENEDICT ARNOLD.

WATERTOWN, May 22, 1775.

Sir:—This Congress have this day received your letter of the 11th instant, informing the Committee of Safety of the reduction of the Fort at *Ticonderoga*, with its dependencies, which was laid before this Congress by said Committee. We applaud the conduct of the troops, and esteem it a very valuable acquisition.

We thank you for your exertions in the cause, and considering the situation of this Colony at this time, having a formidable army in the heart of it, whose motions must be constantly attended to, and as the affairs of that expedition began in the Colony of *Connecticut*, and the cause being common to us all, we have already wrote to the General Assembly of that Colony to take the whole matter respecting the same under their care and direction, until the advice of the Continental Congress can be had in that behalf, a copy of which letter we now enclose to you.

We are, etc."

On the same day, the Massachusetts Committee of Safety laid Arnold's letter of May 11th before the Provincial Congress of that State, and requested that body to "proceed thereon, in such manner as to them in their wisdom shall seem meet," adding the remark, "this Committee apprehend it to be out of their province in any respect whatever." The following is the letter in which the Committee, anticipating Arnold's refusal to yield up his command, relieve themselves of all further responsibility in the matter. This letter shows that Arnold not only had no commission or authority from the *Congress* of Massachusetts, but that all the authority he had was derived from the *Committee of Safety*. Arnold's claim that he was commissioned by the *Congress* of Massachusetts was unfounded. On the 26th of May, the Congress were obliged to call upon the Committee to ascertain the nature and extent of its arrangements with Arnold.

MASSACHUSETTS COMMITTEE OF SAFETY TO BENEDICT ARNOLD.

"CAMBRIDGE, May 28, 1775.

The expedition to Ticonderoga, etc., requiring secrecy, the Congress of this Colony *was not acquainted with the orders you received from this Committee.* It gives us great pleasure to be informed by the express, Captain Brown, that the success you have met with is answerable to your spirit in the undertaking. *We have now to acquaint you that the Congress have taken up this matter, and given the necessary directions respecting these acquisitions. It is then, Sir, become your duty, and is our requirement, that you conform yourself to such advice and orders* as you shall from time to time receive from that body." We are, etc."

NUMBER XXV. Page 69.

The instructions of the Massachusetts Congress to the Committee were dated June 14th. It is evident from their tenor, that Arnold no longer retained the confidence of that Congress, and although he had some time before, while claiming to act under Massachusetts, put himself in direct communication with the Continental Congress, his efforts to secure the confidence of that body had met with no success, for on the 30th of May, immediately after the receipt of a letter from Arnold, stating that he had "certain intelligence" that four hundred regulars were at St. Johns, about to be joined by a large number of Indians, for the purpose of retaking Ticonderoga!" the Continental Congress "ordered that the President, in his letter, acquaint Governor Trumbull that it is the desire of the Congress that he should appoint a person *in whom he can confide, to command the forces at Crown Point and Ticonderoga*."—(*See Journals of Cong.*, 1775, p. 111.)

Colonel Hinman, appointed under this resolution, was on the way to Ticonderoga, with his regiment. Arnold now made another desperate effort to retain the control of affairs on this frontier. On the 13th of June, he addressed a long letter to the Congress at Philadelphia, urging an invasion of Canada. Two weeks before, he had written that the Indians of Canada, with four hundred Regulars, were at St. Johns, on their way to recapture the forts on the lake. Now, he has the "agreeable intelligence that the Indians are determined not to assist the King's troops;" that the "Canadians are very impatient of our delay, and are determined to join us, whenever we appear in the country with any force to support them;" that "Gov. Carleton, by every artifice, has been able to raise only about twenty Canadians," and that if "Congress should think proper to take possession of Montreal and Quebeck, (he is,) I am positive two thousand men might very easily effect it." He then suggests a plan of the expedition, and urges upon Congress the necessity of undertaking it. His letter closes with a "Memorandum:" "Propose, in order to give satisfaction to the different Colonies, that Colonel Hinman's Regiment, now on their march from Connecticut to Ticonderoga, should form part of the army—say one thousand men; 500 do. to be sent from New York, including one company of one hundred men, of the train of artillery, properly equipped; 500 do. *B. Arnold's Regiment, including seamen and marines on board the vessels! (No Green Mountain Boys!*") etc. This letter also contained the agreeable intelligence that the Indians of Canada "have made a law, that if any one of their tribe shall take up arms for that purpose (to assist the King's troops) *he shall immediately be put to death!*"

On the same day, June 13, Arnold wrote the Governor of Connecticut, urging the invasion of Canada, and stating that five chief men of the Indians, "who are now here with their wives and children, and press very hard for our army to march into Canada, as they are much disgusted with the regular troops." Gov. Carleton "is much disgusted with the merchants of Montreal, and has threatened them, if they will not defend the city, in case of an attack, he will set fire to it, and retreat to Quebec."

The extravagance of this letter defeated its purpose. Not the slightest attention was paid to it by Connecticut or the Continental Congress,—their confidence in Arnold no longer existed. The action of the Massachusetts Congress, already mentioned, followed. Its minute instructions to its committee of June 14, plainly show its determination to withdraw all its authority from Arnold, unless, as the instructions stated, "he was willing to continue at one or both of the said posts, *under the command of such chief officer as is, or shall be, appointed by the Government of Connecticut.*" In any other event, the committee was to direct Arnold "to return to this Colony, and render his account of the disposition of the money, ammunition and other things, which he received at his setting out upon his expedition; and also of the charges he has incurred, and the debts which he has contracted in behalf of this Colony, by virtue of the commissions and instructions aforesaid."

When Colonel Hinman's regiment reached Ticonderoga, Arnold was fully advised of the only terms upon which he could continue in the service. His reception and treatment of the committee, therefore, deserves particular mention.

REPORT OF THE CROWN POINT COMMITTEE TO THE MASSACHUSETTS CONGRESS.

CAMBRIDGE, July 6, 1775.

The Committee appointed to proceed to the posts of *Ticonderoga and Crown Point*, etc., beg leave to report, that they proceeded through the new settlements, called the New Hampshire Grants, and carefully observed the road through the same, and find that there is a good road from Williamstown to the place where the road crosseth the river called *Paulet* River, which is about fifteen miles from *Skenesborough;* from thence to the falls of *Wood* Creek, near Major Skene's house, the road is not feasible, and unfit for carriages, but cattle may be drove that way very well.

Your Committee, having taken with them the copies of the commission and instruction from the Committee of Safety to Col. *Benedict Arnold*, and informed themselves, as fully as they were able, in what manner he had executed his said commission and instructions, *and find that he was with Colonel Allen and others at the time the fort was reduced, but do not find that he had any men under his command at the time of the reduction of those fortresses;* but find that he did afterwards possess himself of the sloop on the lake at St. Johns. We find the said

Arnold claiming the command of said sloop and a schooner, which is said to be the property of Major *Skene*, and also all the posts and fortresses at the south end of *Lake Champlain* and *Lake George*, although Colonel *Hinman* was at Ticonderoga with near a thousand men under his command at the several posts.

Your Committee informed the said Arnold of their commission, and, at his request, gave him a copy of their instructions; upon reading of which he seemed greatly discouncerted, and declared he would not be second in command to any person whomsoever; and after some time contemplating upon the matter, resigned his post, and gave your Committee his resignation under his hand, dated the 24th of *June*, 1775, which is herewith submitted, and at the same time ordered his men to be disbanded, which, he said, was between two and three hundred. Your Committee not finding any men regularly under said *Arnold*, by reason of his so disbanding them, appointed Colonel *Easton*, who was then at *Ticonderoga*, to take the command, under Colonel *Hinman*, who was the principal commanding officer of those posts, of the *Connecticut* forces, and endeavored to give the officers and men who had served under said *Arnold* an opportunity to re-engage, of which numbers enlisted, and several of the officers agreed to hold their command under the new appointment.   *   *   *   *   *   *   *   *

Your Committee found that as soon as Col. Arnold had disbanded his men, some of them became dissatisfied and mutinous, and many of them signified to the Committee that they had been informed that they were to be defrauded out of the pay for past services. The Committee, in order to quiet them, engaged under their hands, in behalf of the Colony of *Massachusetts Bay*, that as soon as the rolls should be made up and properly authenticated, they should be paid for their past services, and all those who should engage anew should have the same wages and bounty as is promised to those men who serve within said Colony."
*   *   *   *   *   *   *   *   *   *   *   *

Your Committee, when they had received Col. Arnold's resignation, directed him to return to Congress, and render an account of his proceedings, agreeable to their instructions, a copy of which order is herewith submitted."

The remaining portions of the report have no reference to Arnold. The Committee recognised *Easton* as Colonel, appointed *John Brown* Major, and *Jonas Fay* Surgeon of the Post, and advised the Continental Congress and the New York Convention of the importance of holding Ticonderoga and Crown Point. The following letter from *Edward Mott* to Governor Trumbull supplies some incidents in the Committee's experience which policy would have prohibited them from making public at that time:

"ALBANY, July 6, 1775.

HONORED SIR:—I arrived here last night, ten o'clock, from Ticonderoga; am sent express by Col. *Hinman*, to acquaint the committee at this place, and also the Provincial Congress at *New York*, with the condition of the troops and garrisons at *Ticonderoga, Crown Point* and *Fort George;* expect to set out from hence to *New York* to-morrow; have not as yet waited on the committee here, but write these lines by Captain *Stevens*, who will not tarry, but sets out for home this morning. When I arrived at *Ticonderoga*, Colonel *Hinman* had no command there, as Colonel *Arnold* refused to let him command either of the garrisons, but had given the command of *Ticonderoga* to Captain *Herrick*, from whom Colonel *Hinman's* men were obliged to take their orders, or were not suffered to pass to and from the garrison. The same day, a committee of three gentlemen from *Massachusetts*, viz.: Mr. *Spooner*, Colonel *Foster* and Colonel *Sullivan*, returned to *Ticonderoga* from *Crown Point*, and informed us that they had been to Colonel *Arnold*, with orders from the Congress requiring him to resign the command to Colonel *Hinman*, and that he, with his regiment, should come under the command of said *Hinman*, which said Arnold positively refused; on which the said Committee discharged Colonel *Arnold* from the service, and desired the privilege to speak with the people who had engaged under *Arnold*, but were refused. They further informed that Colonel *Arnold* and some of his people had gone on board the vessels; that they understood they threatened to go to *St. Johns* and deliver the vessels to the Regulars; and that *Arnold* had disbanded all his troops but those that were on board said vessels; that they were treated very ill, and threatened, and after they came away in a batteau, they were fired upon with swivel-guns, and small arms by *Arnold's* people; and that Colonel *Arnold* and his men had got both the vessels, and were drawn off into the lake. On which I desired Colonel *Hinman* to let me, with Lieutenant *Halsey* and Mr. *Duer* (who was Judge of the Court for the County of *Charlotte*, in this Colony), with some men to row, have a batteau, and proceed up the lake, and go on board the vessels. We obtained liberty, and Colonel *Sullivan* consented to go with us. We got on board the vessels about eleven o'clock in the morning, and he confined three of us on board each vessel; men set over us with fixed bayonets, and so kept us till some time in the evening, when we were dismissed and suffered to return. We reasoned with the people on board the vessels all the while we were there, and convinced some of them of their errour, who declared they had been deceived by Colonel *Arnold*. After we returned to the fort, called up Colonel *Hinman*, who ordered Lieutenant *Halsey*, with twenty-five men, to return again to the vessels, and get what people he could on board to join him, and bring one or both vessels to the fort, which was all settled the next day. Colonel Sullivan was much insulted while we were on board the vessels, chiefly by Mr. *Brown*, one of Col. *Arnold's* captains. Captain *Stevens*, who is waiting while I write these lines, will not wait longer, or you should hear more particulars. I expect you will have a full account from the gentlemen committee, after they have laid it before their Congress. Captain *Elijah Babcock* can give a full account of these matters; he tells me he shall be at Hartford in a few days. Shall give further accounts from *New York*. I am, Sir, at command, your Honor's most obedient and humble Servant,

EDWARD MOTT.

To the Hon. Jonathan Trumbull, Esq., Governor."

NUMBER XXVI. Page 83.

The following is Mr. Irving's account of the capture of Ticonderoga, from his "Life of Washington," Vol. I., p. 402-5. It is inserted here as well to justify the statements of the text, as to show the judgment of an impartial and unprejudiced historian upon the general facts relating to the expedition. Although incorrect in some of its minor details, such as the date of the capture of Crown Point, and Arnold's enlistment of men in Western Massachusetts, wherein Mr. Irving has followed Mr. Sparks, the relation generally is as correct as it is vivid and exciting:

"As affairs were now drawing to a crisis, and war was considered inevitable, some bold spirits in Connecticut conceived a project for the outset. This was the surprisal of the old Forts of Ticonderoga and Crown Point, already famous in the French war. Their situation on Lake Champlain gave them the command of the main route to Canada; so that the possession of them would be all-important in case of hostilities. They were feebly garrisoned and negligently guarded, and abundantly furnished with artillery and military stores, so much needed by the patriot army.

"The scheme was set on foot in the purlieus, as it were, of the Provincial Legislature of Connecticut, then in session. It was not openly sanctioned by that body, but secretly favored, and money lent from the treasury to those engaged in it. A committee was appointed, also, to accompany them to the frontier, aid them in raising troops, and exercise over them a degree of superintendance and control.

"Sixteen men were thus enlisted in Connecticut, a greater number in Massachusetts, but the greatest accession of force was from what was called the "New Hampshire Grants." This was a region having the Connecticut River on one side, and Lake Champlain and the Hudson River on the other,—being, in fact, the country forming the present State of Vermont. It had long been a disputed territory, claimed by New York and New Hampshire. George II. had decided in favor of New York, but the Governor of New Hampshire had made grants of between one and two hundred townships in it, whence it had acquired the name of the New Hampshire Grants. The settlers on these Grants resisted the attempts of New York to eject them, and formed themselves into an association called "The Green Mountain Boys." Resolute, strong-handed fellows they were, with Ethan Allen at their head, a native of Connecticut, but brought up among the Green Mountains. He and his Lieutenants, Seth Warner and Remember Baker, were outlawed by the Legislature of New York, and rewards offered for their apprehension. They and their associates armed themselves, set New York at defiance, and swore they would be the death of any one who should attempt their arrest.

"Thus Ethan Allen was becoming a kind of Robin Hood among the mountains, when the present crisis changed the relative position of things, as if by magic. Boundary feuds were forgotten amid the great questions of Colonial rights. Ethan Allen at once stepped forward, a patriot, and volunteered, with his Green Mountain Boys, to serve in the popular cause. He was well fitted for the enterprise in question, by his experience as a frontier champion, his robustness of mind and body, and his fearless spirit. He had a rough eloquence, also, that was very effective with his followers. 'His style,' says one who knew him personally, 'was a singular compound of local barbarisms, scriptural phrases and oriental wildness; and although unclassic, and sometimes ungrammatical, was highly animated and forcible.' Washington, in one of his letters, says there was 'an original something in him which commanded admiration!'

"Thus reinforced, the party, now two hundred and seventy strong, pushed forward to Castleton, a place within a few miles of the head of Lake Champlain. Here a council of war was held on the 2d (8th?) of May. Ethan Allen was placed at the head of the expedition, and James Easton and Seth Warner as second and third in command. Detachments were sent off to Skenesborough, (now Whitehall,) and another place on the lake, with orders to seize all the boats they could find, and bring them to Shoreham, opposite Ticonderoga, whither Allen prepared to proceed with the main body.

"At this juncture, another adventurous spirit arrived at Castleton. This was Benedict Arnold, since so sadly renowned. He, too, had conceived the project of surprising Ticonderoga and Crown Point; *or, perhaps, had caught the idea from its first agitators in Connecticut,* in the militia of which Province he held a captain's commission. He had proposed the scheme to the Massachusetts Committee of Safety. It had met with their approbation. They had given him a Colonel's commission; authorized him to raise a force in Western Massachusetts, not exceeding four hundred men, and furnished him with money and means. Arnold had enlisted but a few officers and men, when he heard of the expedition from Connecticut being on the march. He instantly hurried on, with one attendant, to overtake it, leaving his few recruits to follow as best they could. In this way he reached Castleton, just after the council of war.

"Producing the Colonel's commission received from the Massachusetts Committee of Safety, he now aspired to the supreme command. His claims were disregarded by the Green Mountain Boys; they would follow no leader but Ethan Allen. As they formed the majority of the party, Arnold was fain to acquiesce, and serve as a volunteer, with the rank, but not the command, of Colonel.

"The party arrived at Shoreham, opposite Ticonderoga, on the night of the 9th of May. The detachment sent in quest of boats, had failed to arrive. There were a few boats at hand, with which the transportation was commenced. It was slow work; the night wore away; day was about to break, and but eighty-three men, with Allen and Arnold, had crossed. Should they wait for the residue, day would dawn, the garrison wake, and their enterprise might fail. Allen drew up his men, addressed them in his own emphatic style, and announced his intention to make a dash at the fort, without waiting for more force. 'It is a desperate attempt,' said he; 'and I ask no man to go against his will. I will take the lead, and be the first to advance. You that are willing to follow, poise your firelocks.' Not a firelock but was poised.

"They mounted the hill briskly, but in silence, guided by a boy from the neighborhood. The day dawned as Allen arrived at a sally-port. A sentry pulled trigger on him, but his piece missed fire. He retreated through a covered way. Allen and his men followed. Another sentry thrust at Easton with his bayonet, but was struck down by Allen, and begged for quarter. It was granted on condition of his leading the way, instantly to the quarters of the Commandant, Capt. Delaplace, who was yet in bed. Being arrived there, Allen thundered at the door, and demanded a surrender of the fort. By this time his followers had formed into two lines on the parade ground, and given three hearty cheers. The Commandant appeared at his door, half dressed, "the frightened face of his pretty wife peering over his shoulder.' He gazed at Allen in bewildered astonishment. 'By whose authority do you act?' exclaimed he. 'In the name of the Great Jehovah, and the Continental Congress!' replied Allen, with a flourish of his sword, and an oath, which we do not care to subjoin.

"There was no disputing the point. The garrison, like the commander, had been startled from sleep, and made prisoners as they rushed forth in their confusion. A surrender accordingly took place. The captain, and forty-eight men, which composed the garrison, were sent prisoners to Hartford, in Connecticut. A great supply of military and naval stores, so important in the present crisis, was found in the fortress.

"Colonel Seth Warner, who had brought over the residue of the party from Shoreham, was now sent with a detachment against Crown Point, which surrendered on the 12th of May, without firing a gun. Here were taken upward of a hundred cannon.

"Arnold now insisted vehemently on his right to command Ticonderoga; being, as he said, the only officer invested with legal authority. His claims had again to yield to the superior popularity of Ethan Allen, to whom the Connecticut Committee, which had accompanied the enterprise, gave an instrument in writing, investing him with the command of the fortress and its dependencies, until he should receive the orders of the Connecticut Assembly or the Continental Congress. Arnold, while forced to acquiesce, sent a protest, and a statement of his grievances to the Massachusetts Legislature. * * * * *

"Thus a partisan band, unpractised in the art of war, had, by a series of daring exploits, and almost without the loss of a man, won for the patriots the command of Lakes George and Champlain, and thrown open the great highway to Canada.

www.ingramcontent.com/pod-product-compliance
Lightning Source LLC
Chambersburg PA
CBHW020120170426
43199CB00009B/570